FRONTIER TO CITY

FRONTIER TO CITY
LIVERMORE
CALIFORNIA

ALAN M. FRANK

AMERICA
THROUGH
TIME

I would like to dedicate this to my wife, Peggy,

who put up with my endless sitting at my desk and computer.

America Through Time
www.through-time.com

First published 2025
Copyright © Alan M. Frank 2025

ISBN 978-1-63499-510-8

Typeset in 10.5pt on 13pt Sabon
Printed and bound in England

PREFACE

This book is an overview of the evolution of the City of Livermore from the Spanish Alta California frontier. This story is in many ways comparable to the development of several towns and cities along the rail lines in the west, especially those in formerly Spanish-governed areas. The railroads being built across privately owned land had a rule that if an owner wanted a station at a given location, he had to give the railroad the necessary property. This was the general practice in California and elsewhere from the 1860s into the twentieth century.

Livermore, California, emerged and grew around privately owned, barren land given to the first Transcontinental Railroad in 1869. Tucson, Arizona, is a good example of similar development, paralleling the Southern Pacific Railroad which opened in 1880. Historic Albuquerque, New Mexico, did not give property to the Santa Fe Railroad. Consequently, Albuquerque station and the city center were built and remain several miles away from the old town.

The book aims to illustrate the sociological and financial perspectives of Livermore's development and is structured about various eras but not entirely linear in time. The chapters essentially represent the eras. Issues originating in a particular era are occasionally described in other chapters where they are important.

Information on key events and issues was often gleaned from secondary or incomplete multiple sources. I make no claim that descriptions of events, and especially dates, are completely accurate. What is important is the juxtaposition and interaction of the events to the town, the region, and the nation. Important dates are presented to provide a reference to the historic evolution. Many newspaper articles are referenced by the date of publication rather than that of the event. Often the date of events described are not evident. References in the endnotes generally give dates of a publication. The articles illustrate the tenor of the time thus precise dates may not be necessary.

Newspapers and the archives of Livermore Heritage Guild (LHG) provided much source information. Particularly helpful were the late Barbara Bunshah's indices of Livermore newspaper articles from the earliest papers published in 1874. Most of those newspapers are on microfilm. They are available at the Livermore Library and LHG. Missing from the microfilms and catalog are sporadic copies of the *Livermore Herald* from 1877 to 1899, the *Echo* from 1882 to 1887, and the *Livermore Independent*. The University of California's digital newspaper collection available online was also extremely helpful.

Like many museums, LHG has an extensive collection of historic materials, much of which is awaiting cataloging by part-time, volunteer members. Articles by members or former members are in the collection. Though not necessarily yet on the website, they are on file. Some were provided to me by the former City Historian Don Meeker and LHG Librarian Linda Driver. Much was found by me in the many hours of digging through the back rooms of LHG's museum in the old Carnegie Library.

Newspaper articles mention significant events but do not necessarily record public leanings. LHG has been recording historic interviews since the early 1980s. Early interviews were recorded on tape and more recently, digitally. Several, though not all, audio recordings are available on LHG's website. Some have been transcribed and the printed text is available in the LHG library. A recorded oral history by Herbert Hagemann (1985) was transcribed by Linda Driver and is quoted. Audio of Anita Gandolfo (2023), John "Jack" Jensen (1981), and Francis May Baer Santucci (1982), but not transcribed, are also quoted.

Published books and articles were also quite helpful, especially for the early eras. Recorded and interpersonal discussions contributed more recent information. Ann Marshall Homan's book *Historic Livermore, California: Illustrated A to Z* provided much detailed information about important individuals, their families and local organizations. The book *Early Livermore*, published by LHG in 2006, is an extensive collection of historic images and photographs from LHG's archives. Photos of structures, people, and events mentioned but not shown herein are available in *Early Livermore*.

Many published books provided details of the general issues surrounding railroad history and the Transcontinental Railroad. Those references are listed in the endnotes and bibliography. They mostly do not describe the history of the portion of the railroad through Livermore.

Images of the Associates of the Central Pacific Railroad are presented in almost every history and website of the building of the Transcontinental Railroad. They had almost no personal connection to the town other than passing through on the train. Images of other principles in the development and functioning of the railroads are also commonly available. Consequently, publishing them in this volume would be considered extraneous.

I wish to thank LHG members who were particularly helpful and supportive, including Jeff and Loretta Kaskey, Will Bolton, Harry Briley, Linda Driver, Richard Finn, Susan Junk, Don Meeker, and Anna Siig. Special thanks to Loretta Kaskey, for research of the Mendenhall property acquisition and finding a copy of the original Livermore Plat as recorded. Many thanks also to Don Meeker for much useful information, especially in providing transcribed copies of early handwritten town records, as well as his work making the newspaper collections accessible for research.

I also wish to recognize the support of and multiple discussions with current Livermore Mayor John Marchand, the late former Mayor Dr. John Shirley, former Mayor Cathy Brown, former City Manager Mark Roberts, and Reverend William Nebo, retired, of the First Presbyterian Church.

Many others have contributed through the years to the information for this book. They include Jim Allen, Henry Bender, Jim Concannon, Ralph Domenici, Gary Drummond, Dottie Eberly, Mel Lemos, Arthur Lloyd, Steve Rusconi, John Sarboraria, Barry Schrader, Robert Searle, and James Swofford.

I especially wish to thank Fonthill Media, Carol Jensen, and my editor Karel Ancona for all their detailed help and support.

In my fifty years as a Livermore resident, I have had many discussions with members of the major demographics and sociological groups within the city. My long-time membership of the Rotary Club of Livermore, as well as LHG have been key resources in this regard.

Alan Frank

CONTENTS

VALLE DE SAN JOSÉ, LAS POSITAS

The Valle de San José, now called the Livermore valley, is completely surrounded by hills and mountains. It is a gentle sloping plain, irregular in shape. Its greatest length is 14 miles, and its width varies from 4–8 miles north and south. Trails through the valley were originally footpaths used for centuries by the Ohlone and other regional tribes.

The Seunen and Sacalane were Ohlone tribelets settled in small villages in the valley. The tribelets were separate, but they traded and intermarried. They developed their own dialects of the Ohlone language. They were generally peaceful and were stable for hundreds, perhaps thousands of years.

The Ohlone were a Stone Age hunting and gathering society. Wildlife, from grasshoppers to bears, were such sufficient food sources that the tribelets in the valley never needed to do any farming. They used bow and arrow for hunting larger animals. Bones, antlers, and stones were fashioned into tools and arrowheads. Animal skins were used for blankets and clothing. A local tribal legend was that prairie falcons in the area originated on Brushy Peak on the north side of the valley.

Oak trees were common in the valley, and large amounts of acorns were gathered and stored over the winter. They were ground into a flour using stone tools and then prepared as a non-meat addition to their diet. Seeds of grasses and mustard, as well as nuts and berries, were seasonally gathered and consumed. Reeds collected from wet areas were used for making baskets and arrow shafts.[1]

The earliest record of any Europeans visiting the Valle de San José, is the account of an expedition of Captain Pedro Fages, a platoon of soldiers, and Missionary Juan Crespi in April 1772. Fagas, previously a member of Gaspar de Portolá's 1769–1870 expedition, was the commander for northern Alta California. Crespi described his first encounters with the natives in the valley:

> … numerous villages of very gentile and peaceful heathen, many of fair complexion. It is a very suitable place for a good mission, having good lands, much water, fire wood and many heathen. We stopped here a little while, surprised to see some seventy heathen, not counting the women, boys, girls, because they were very tall, fair and white. We gave them some beads, and concluded that in some words were the same as the language spoken at Monterrey.[2]

Mission San José was founded a generation after the Fages and Crespi expedition by the Franciscan Father Fermin Lasuén in 1797. Trouble began with the mission's zeal to convert natives. Many members of the Ohlone tribelets residing in the valley were taken to Mission San José. They were required to be baptized and forced, virtually enslaved, into brutal labor for the mission.[3] Their customs were banned, they were not permitted any freedoms, and some trying to leave were executed. The converted natives were forced to join Spanish soldiers to baptize the remaining natives in the valley and bring back those who had run away.[4] The Valle de San José was part of the Mission de San José, where it was used for cattle grazing. Aristocrat Juan Francisco Bernal and his family managed cattle ranching for the mission. Converted natives became vaqueros for the mission rancho.

Two Sacalanes tried to stir up a revolt of the Mission San José Christian natives. Governor Diego de Borica of Alta California ordered Sergeant Pedro Amador to take two soldiers and twenty civilians into the valley to capture the chiefs and return baptized natives. They met considerable resistance, and the village was destroyed. About thirty villagers were captured. The other two Sacalane villages in the valley were quickly abandoned. Only two members were captured while the remainder sought refuge in the hills.[5] Punitive expeditions continued for almost another twenty years.

Some of those who did manage to leave the mission settled in the hills and raided the white settlements for horses and cattle. Many were decimated by smallpox brought in by the Spanish. Many of the *vaqueros* left the mission after Mexican independence and the secularization of the natives of many tribes and tribal groups in the Bay Area, so those that left were of mixed family heritage.[6] It was estimated that twenty years after Crespi's expedition, only 50 percent of the natives remained.[7] The combination of the mission's activities and the smallpox significantly reduced the native population. The 1870 census indicated only about 110 natives remained in the valley.[8] The Mexican War of Independence ended with the defeat of the Spanish army in 1821. The defeat effectively ended Spanish rule of Mexico. A Mexican republic and congress established in 1824 supported secularization of the missions' vast territories and rules. They encouraged citizens to settle the former mission lands. The mission friars were mostly Spanish and rebelled against the secularization decrees of the Mexican government. There were several failed Spanish attempts to reconquer Mexico. Mexico's independence was finally recognized by Spain in 1836. Settlers were able to apply to the Mexican government for formal land grants of former mission *rancheros*. They were required to be Mexican citizens and live on and work their property. *Ranchero* property lines were claimed and agreed upon by settlers. The lines were only loosely defined in the *diseño*, or property description, of the application.[9] They ranged in size from 1–11 square leagues. On most of the *ranchos*, the main industry was that of cattle raising, though some farming was done to support the herds and household needs.

Robert Livermore was born in Springfield in Essex, England, in 1799 and was baptized Protestant. He initially apprenticed as a mason and then went to sea at age seventeen. He served in the British fleet under Lord Cochrane with the objective of freeing Peru from Spanish domination. He subsequently served on the merchant ship *Colonel Young* which brought him to California, likely shortly before Mexican independence. The exact year is not known because dates of ship landings were falsified during the War for Independence. He apparently left the ship in San Pedro and worked his way to Monterey. He became a Mexican citizen and was baptized Catholic at Mission Santa Clara. He worked at several different *rancheros*. For a time, he was the majordomo of Rancho de la Torre near Monterey.

These *rancheros* were usually quite a distance from one another so that each individual ranchero became a social and economic unit and some a religious unit. Each *ranchero* was a frontier settlement and became small communities. The European population of Alta California was less than 4,000 at the time. Using his skills as a mason, he helped José Amador build the first house in the valley. Amador later returned the favor by helping Livermore build his house.[10]

Blacksmith William Gulnac settled in the valley he called the Rancho Del Valle de San José. He was awarded an early Mexican land grant in 1834. Gulnac married and moved to San José, thereby giving up his grant by no longer living on the property.[11]

Livermore began ranching in the valley around 1827, although he had no legal title to it at the time. Livermore married Josefa Higuera in 1838, a widow with one daughter, whom he had met at Rancho Agua Caliente, her father's *ranchero*, a few years before. She was a great-granddaughter

Robert Livermore, 1799–1858. This image is dated 1835. The photo hung in the Bank of Italy and was given to the library in 1929. It has been published on many occasions since then. (*Livermore Heritage Guild*)

of Juan Francisco Bernal.[12] Livermore moved his family to the present Sunol Valley and made trips from there to the valley.[13] The following year, Livermore and Noriega, with Amador's help, built an adobe house near what became known as Las Positas Creek.[14]

The natives in the hills were occasionally troublesome, stealing cattle and horses. Whenever they raided, Livermore retreated with his family to Amador's Rancho for protection because it was rarely molested.[15]

José Noriega and Livermore were both Mexican citizens and filed a joint application for a land grant. They received the grant for northern and eastern portions of the Valle de San José in 1840. The land was split between them with Noriega calling his western segment Rancho Santa Rita.

Livermore named the eastern segment and adjacent hills Rancho las Positas del Valle de San José. Rancho Las Positas lies between the Diablo Range and East Bay hills. He derived the name, Las Positas, from the Spanish word "*pozos*" meaning springs. There was a creek running through the property and several nearby springs.

Livermore's *rancho* was at the crossroads of wagon trails from the Bay Area to the Central Valley. The surrounding hills isolated it from developing towns in nearby Alta California.

The southwestern portion of the valley was granted to the four descendants of Juan Francisco Bernal, José Agostin Bernal, Juan Pablo

The 1839 Diseño, which is the property description for the joint land grant application of partners Jose Noriega and Roberto Livermore. (*Bancroft Library*)

Bernal, Antonio María Pico, and Antonio Sunol who retained the name Rancho el Valle de San José.

English-speaking settlers from the East were arriving into Spanish-speaking Mexican territory. The United States was at war with Mexico, and the settlers from the East were rebelling against Mexican rule. Robert Livermore was the only bilingual speaker in the valley and was sought after for directions and advice.

Rancho Las Positas, at the foot of what became known as Livermore Pass, was a convenient way station on the trail from Stockton to Mission San José. It was also the junction of the Dublin and Patterson Pass wagon roads. Rancho las Positas was a self-sufficient frontier settlement. Cattle, sheep, and horse ranching was sustained by dry land crops for feed and domestic consumption. Alta California was sparsely populated, and good farming and ranching land was attracting settlers from the Eastern U.S.

Most ranchers ventured off their land by wagon perhaps only once a year to bring their products to market and procure needed supplies. The local economy was dominated by trade with self-sufficient settlers having little or no significant money. Livermore raised apples, pears, olives, and a small amount of wheat for domestic purposes. He also had a small vineyard and was later said to have made his own wine.[16]

Wagons could not carry profitable amounts of grain across the hills to markets. Driving large numbers of cattle and sheep to market was also not profitable as they likely could not all be sold at once. A wagon or two of the higher-value ranch products, such as hides, leather, wool, and tallow, rather than meat, brought in sufficient trade and income. Hauling a heavily loaded wagon across the hills was slow going, so the trip to San Jose, Oakland, or Stockton markets could take a week or more.

William Mendenhall, born in Green County, Ohio, came to California by wagon train with a party of eleven men including his brothers. The number of Eastern settlers were beginning to outnumber the Mexican population at the time of his arrival. He quickly became involved in the rebel Bear Flaggers, who were seeking independence from Mexico. When the U.S. declared war with Mexico, he joined John C. Fremont's California battalion. His first meeting with Livermore was when the battalion camped at Rancho Las Positas.[17]

The 1840s were a tumultuous time in California history. The U.S. was then at war with Mexico, and the settlers from the East were rebelling against Mexican rule. The Treaty of Guadalupe Hidalgo ended the war with Mexico in 1848, and ceded California, much of Colorado, Arizona, and New Mexico to the U.S. A term of the treaty was to recognize and preserve the property rights of the Spanish and Mexican citizens of Alta

William and Mary Allen Mendenhall, married in 1847. Photo *circa* 1895. (*Livermore Heritage Guild*)

California and the Mexican land grants in the region. Gold was discovered in California in the year after the treaty.

The Spanish brought horses to the Americas. Many were released or escaped in the years since they arrived. The horses had no natural enemies, resulting in large wild herds in Alta California during the mission period. The Murrieta brothers annually rounded up a couple of hundred horses in the hills around the Valle de San José. They generally drove them south to sell to Mexican settlers. They regularly stayed and held rodeos on Rancho Las Positas until the 1850s. An artesian well south of town fed their horses. Today, the well serves the Murrieta's Well winery. Joaquin Murrieta became an outlaw after he was forced off his gold mine claim by anti-Mexican discrimination and a California tax in violation of the Treaty of Guadalupe Hidalgo.

The industrial revolution had hardly made its way west to California, and almost not at all for the *rancheros*. Transportation of people and goods for long distances was only by horse, wagon, or ship. These had marginally improved over many centuries. Trails were converted to roads. Ships increased in size and could carry more than wagons but only from port to port. In the U.S., canals were built to carry people and goods from the East Coast ports to the Midwest.

The discovery of gold changed everything for California. During the gold rush, Las Positas became a first-day stopover for those headed for the Gold Country. Many arrived in San Francisco by ship and headed for

Joaquin Murietta. (*California State Library*)

the hills on fast horses, anxious for riches. Nearby cities grew quickly, especially those on navigable waterways such as San Francisco, Oakland, Stockton, and Sacramento. Rancho Las Positas was about equal distance from San Jose, Stockton, and Oakland. However, for Las Positas, the annual trek with heavy wagons to the nearest cities was still at least a week-long affair. The gold also created the fortunes for the business leaders of San Francisco and Sacramento.

The Valle de San José became known as the Livermore Valley and was included in Murray Township in eastern Alameda County when they were established in 1853.[18]

Mexican residents had their own gold-mining claims and properties, whose rights were supposed to be protected by the two-year-old treaty. With the growing political strength of the settlers, the Mexican citizens were driven from their claims. A tax was created for "non-American" miners as soon as California became a state. The tax included natives as well as former Mexican citizens, despite the protections in the treaty.

Governor Peter Barnett was quoted that "a war of extermination would be waged until the Indian race should become extinct," and that, "It was beyond the power and wisdom of man to avert the inevitable destiny."[19]

The Stockton House was a building owned by Livermore on his property. It was a cantina operated by Yreneo "Don" Ramirez. It often attracted *bandidos* to plan their escapades in the decade after gold was discovered.[20] Joaquin Murrieta, forced off his claim, became a desperado. He, his brother, and a few followers robbed miners and stole their horses. He helped support the poor and was regarded by some as the Spanish Robin Hood. With a hideout in Alameda Canõn, he likely crossed Las Positas on many occasions. It was said his gang "stole over one-hundred-thousand-dollars worth of gold and killed nineteen men." He was finally gunned down by rangers.

Chemist William Henry Brewer, working for the California State Geological Survey, explored the valley and surrounding hills in the early 1860s. His journal details the mineralogy which identified possible mining sites.[21] He also noted there were more dogs than people in the valley.

Geologists say that Livermore Valley was several times submerged and many marine fossil remains are found. The distribution of soils was affected by these floods. Edwin Bryant noted:

A *carretado* (cart-load) of fossil oyster shells were shown me by Mr. Livermore, which had been hauled for the purpose of being manufactured into lime. Some of these shells were eight inches in length, and of corresponding breadth and thickness. They were dug from a hill two or three miles distant, which is composed almost entirely of this fossil.

Several bones belonging to the skeleton of a whale, discovered by Mr. Livermore on the summit of one of the highest elevations in the vicinity of his residence, were shown to me. The skeleton, when discovered, was nearly perfect and entirely exposed, and its elevation above the level of the sea between one and two thousand feet.[22]

Wildlife in the area included grizzly and black bears, deer and elk, puma (mountain lion) and lynx, and many game birds. They attracted many hunters, especially before the infilling of ranches which reduced their numbers. Mountaineer and bear hunter James Adams came to the valley to hunt in the surrounding hills and Corral Hollow during the mid-1850s. He captured and tamed several grizzly bears, which were exhibited in San Francisco and then in Barnum's circus in New York. It gained him the moniker Grizzly Adams.[23]

Prospectors based in the area combed the hills for profitable mineral deposits. A coal seam was found by Francis O'Burne in the hills just east of Las Positas.[24] He proposed building a railroad to bring the coal to market. He bought an easement for a 400-foot right-of-way across Las Positas from Livermore for $5. The easement would remain valid only if railroad construction began within two years.[25] Later coal discoveries in Corral Hollow on the east side of the Diablo Range became more profitable with access to the river and later railroads. Coal mines and oil and gas wells on the west side of the Diablo range were eventually commercialized.

Livermore died on February 14, 1858.[26] Portions of Rancho Las Positas were willed to his children and surveyed. Their holdings were Robert, Jr., 448 acres; Carlota, 396 acres; and Miligras, 969 acres.[27] No railroad was built across Rancho Las Positas during Livermore's lifetime.

Transportation and communication across the country had improved but were still slow.

2

RAILROAD DEALS, SHENANIGANS, AND TRANSCONTINENTAL CHALLENGES

Histories of the Transcontinental Railroad abound, though little has been written about bringing the railroad to the Bay Area.[1] The Central Pacific Railroad (CP) was chartered to build east from Sacramento with no intent of coming to the Bay Area from Sacramento and through the Livermore valley. The bringing of the Transcontinental Railroad through Livermore valley was a complex process of deals, shenanigans, and illegal activities. The business of the railroads through Livermore has both directly and indirectly impacted the town and city throughout its existence.

The railroad ushered in a new era for the Valley as well as the rest of California. It created the conditions that originated the town and its economy. Many of the changes the railroad initiated had already occurred in much of the East and had not yet occurred in the remainder of the West. Railroads were a major driver, a revolution, not only in transportation but also agriculture, industrialization, and the ways of doing business.

Railroad mania was sweeping the country but was late coming to California. Many miles of prairie, mountains, deserts, and hostile natives separated California from the rest of the country. Travel to California was difficult, dangerous, and time consuming. Wagon trains could take several months from the Missouri River. It was a long, slow journey for ships sailing around the Cape Horn. The Butterfield Mail Stage made the trip in three to four weeks. Passengers traveling by steamship to and from the East Coast via Central America took about the same time. That route required a perilous crossing of disease-infested jungle. The threat of contracting malaria or yellow fever while crossing Panama or Nicaragua was significant. Heavy equipment had to be shipped to California by sail around Cape Horn.

Asa Whitney, a successful international dry-goods merchant, traveled from the East Coast to China by ship. During his arduous return sea voyage, he devised a concept of building a railroad across the country to the West Coast, with the purpose of easing the trade route to China. His China trade made him wealthy, and he proposed financing the railroad with the sale of adjacent land to underwrite the project.[2]

East Coast railroads were building to the Midwest, and the West Coast was not yet part of the country; in 1846, the U.S. was at war with Mexico. However, negotiations with Britain over the Oregon Territory were nearing final approval.

Whitney's plan was not necessarily the first suggestion of a Pacific Railroad, but it was well-presented to Congress. He requested Congress authorize a survey of the route. Questions even arose whether the U.S. Constitution allowed federal support of infrastructure endeavors. He proposed a bill to Congress for a northern route to Oregon in 1846. Oregon was the major destination of settlers from the East before the California gold rush. Whitney's proposal was opposed by Tennessee Senator Thomas Hart Benton, a leader of the Southern obstructionists, which caused Whitney's proposal to languish. Whitney eventually saw his dream for a Pacific railroad come to fruition nearly twenty-five years later.

The Treaty of Guadalupe Hidalgo ended the war with Mexico in 1848. California gold was discovered the following year, becoming a major driver of commercial development and needed to be protected. For both military and commercial reasons, the concept of a railroad to the Pacific was finally in the forefront. Congress authorized Jefferson Davis, the secretary of war, to survey possible routes for a Pacific Railway in 1853.[3] Five military survey parties were established and given general instructions to explore regions that might be suitable for railroads. A map prepared for the survey indicated either established settler's trails or routes explored by Fremont. Extensive blank areas of the map indicated how much of the country was still unexplored.

A survey party from the state capital at Benicia, led by Lt. R. S. Williamson, camped on Livermore's property. Williamson's report concluded that the path across Livermore's Pass over the Diablo Range and through Alameda Cañon was the best dry-land route from the Central Valley to the San Francisco Bay Area.[4] Charles Koppel, the assistant civil engineer and artist of the Williamson party, sketched the entrance to Livermore Pass.[5]

The surveys identified five possible transcontinental routes to the West Coast between Canada and Mexico all of which were eventually surveyed and built out. The southernmost routes passed through what was then considered Mexican territory. Obstructionists in Congress from the Southern states prevented a specific route from being adopted and the establishment of a Pacific Railroad bill.

Charles Koppel's sketch of the entrance to Livermore Pass. The horses at the far left are entering the pass. Interstate 580 now passes between the hills on the right. The sketch was made near today's Greenville Road. (*National Archives, Pacific Railroad Survey, 1853*)

A group of San Francisco investors, including army captain and bank manager William Tecumseh Sherman, organized the Sacramento Valley Railroad. It was to connect the rich placer developments in the Sierra foothills with Sacramento. Railroad design engineer Theodore Judah was brought from New York to build the railroad in 1854, which commenced service two years later.[6]

The Sacramento Valley Railroad was the first steam railroad west of the Rockies but was not financially successful. The economic failure of the Sacramento Valley Railroad initially made the investors reluctant to back another mountain railroad.

Judah devised a plan and published a book, *A Practical Plan for Building a Pacific Railroad*, in 1857.[7] At that time, there was no standard gauge, which is the separation between the rails. The most common gauges were the British standard of 4 feet, 8½ inches in the north, but 5 feet in the south. Judah suggested in his book that the line have four rails. The inner two rails would have a standard gauge and the outer two would be about 16 feet apart. This would allow car widths of more than 20 feet. The wider gauge would make trains more stable, and with much larger locomotives, it would allow them to run at a speed of 100 mph. The larger cars would have wheels on all four rails, allowing much heavier freight capabilities and greater passenger comfort.

Judah lobbied Congress for a federal project to build a railroad to the Pacific. After publishing his book, he became known as "Judah the dreamer," subsequently "crazy Judah." He convinced the California legislature of the need for a Pacific Railway. He crafted a bill and returned to Washington with a delegation of California legislators. Judah presented his bill to President James Buchanan to no avail. The route could not be chosen because of the north–south standoff in Congress.[8]

Senator Abraham Lincoln and railroad builder Grenville Dodge met in August 1859 in Council Bluffs, Iowa. They expressed their preference for the central route via the Livermore Valley and across the Sierra. Lincoln apparently said there were more important issues at hand. However, the Pacific Railroad became a plank in the Republican platform of the 1860 presidential election:[9]

> That a railroad to the Pacific Ocean is imperatively demanded by the interests of the whole country; that the federal government ought to render immediate and sufficient aid in its construction; as preliminary thereto, a daily overland mail should be promptly established.[10] [The daily Overland Mail Company became the Pony Express.]

None of the survey parties identified a pass across the Sierra. Returning to California, Judah set himself to exploring the Sierra with a party of surveyors to find a reasonable route in 1860. At Dutch Flat, a bustling mining town, he met the druggist Dr. Daniel Strong who showed him the so-called Dutch Flat route via Donner Summit. From Donner Summit, Judah saw the Tahoe Canyon, which cut through the second ridge. His reconnaissance proved that a railroad could cross the Sierra, climbing over a single summit with grades of no more than 100 feet per mile or 1.8 percent.[11]

In Sacramento, a jubilant Judah had several meetings with potential investors to sell stock for his Central Pacific Railroad (CP), touting the discovery of the route. Strong later claimed he found the route he called the Dutch Flat route. He attended one meeting in November, reporting more than thirty people in attendance and encouraged seven from the meeting to subscribe to fund Judah's detailed survey of the proposed route. By the spring of 1861, the Central Pacific Railroad of California (CP) was incorporated to build east from Sacramento to the California border.

Eleven were named to the board of directors and committed to buy 150 shares of company stock at $100 each. All of the board members were from Sacramento and nearby mining towns and were the original contributors and purchasers of the shares necessary to make the legal requirement for incorporation.[12]

Judah, Leland Stanford, Collis Huntington, Mark Hopkins, Judge Edward Crocker and brother Charles Crocker became the principal directors of the company. Stanford, who had just been nominated for governor, was made president at Judah's suggestion. Huntington became vice president but resented not being made president.[13]

After the deaths of Judah and Judge Crocker, the remainder became known as the Big Four or the Associates. The Big Four were shopkeepers in Sacramento and did well supplying the gold miners.

Official selection of the rail route did not occur until after Lincoln became president. Lincoln's election opened a period of intense lobbying. The secession of the South eliminated votes opposing Lincoln's preference led to the signing of the Pacific Railroad Act on July 1, 1862. The bill also set the standard gauge at 4 feet, 8½ inches. While Judah was back lobbying Congress, Huntington was sent to New York as an agent for the CP to act in its best interest and to raise money for the cause.[14]

A group of San Francisco investors incorporated in 1860 and commenced construction of the San Francisco & San Jose Railroad (SF&SJ), today's Peninsula line. Their board included Judge Timothy Dame, Peter Donahue, Alexander Houston, and others. They hired Charles McLaughlin's construction firm to build the line. The initial portion of the line opened in 1863 and was completed in 1864. The SF&SJ directors proposed extending the SF&SJ east through Alameda Canõn, the Livermore Valley and to Sacramento, thus providing rail access to San Francisco.

Stanford met with San Francisco investors in an attempt to raise money for the Central Pacific. He came away with nothing because the CP was only chartered to build east from Sacramento and not to service San Francisco.

Throughout the spring of 1862, Judah, with the help of Congressman Aaron Sargent, composed a bill to present to Congress. The bill would charter the CP to build east from Sacramento and the Union Pacific (UP) to build west from the Missouri River.

Judah reported to the Associates that officers of the SF&SJ had been lobbying to build the railroad connecting to San Francisco rather than Sacramento as stated in Judah's proposed bill.

The SF&SJ had the advantage in that they were actively constructing the line to San Jose, whereas the CP had not constructed any rail at all. Hearing the SF&SJ had sent principals to join the fray, the Associates redirected Huntington from New York to Washington with full power of attorney, to support Judah's bill.

The SF&SJ principles threatened to kill the CP bill if it did not serve San Francisco.[15] Huntington sought to compromise with the San Francisco group by allowing them to build from Sacramento to San Francisco. The segment was never in the CP charter or the proposed bill as such. Huntington also agreed to changing the wording of the bill, from "build east from Sacramento" to "east from Pacific tidal waters."

The withdrawal from Congress of the secessionist states eliminated most opposing votes. The bill was passed with a vote in the House of 79 to 49 and Senate by 35 to 5. The Pacific Railroad Act, signed by President Lincoln on July 1, 1862, defined the central route for a railroad and telegraph line from the Missouri River to the Pacific tide waters.

Huntington secretly agreed to assign to the WP principals, as individuals, any property rights that might be conferred by the government. Most properties along the route of the WP were supposedly protected by the terms of the Treaty of Guadalupe Hidalgo. Little of the property was legally subject to the government's land grants for the builders because of the treaty. Thus, the property rights were not considered particularly valuable.

Together they proposed a new company called the Western Pacific Railroad (WP), to build from San Jose to Sacramento, thus connecting to San Francisco via the SF&SJ. The WP was to be managed and supported by the SF&SJ. The formal terms of the agreement defined the WP route.

No funds were committed or transferred at the time. It alleviated the threat to kill the bill should the segment not be included in the act. The agreement with the SF&SJ remained secret until the WP was included, and San Francisco was recognized by the government as the western terminus of the railroad in an addendum to the initial bill passed three years later.[16]

Items in the CP, SF&SJ agreement, though innocuous at the time, gave Huntington a significant future advantage over the San Francisco investors. The river to Sacramento is Pacific tidal water. Identification of the western terminus as Pacific tide water in the bill could be interpreted as Sacramento, San Francisco, or somewhere in between.

Huntington's agreement to create the WP carried a requirement to build 25 miles a year. A stipulation of the agreement with the CP was that should the WP fail to meet the conditions, ownership of the company, including rolling stock and other appurtenances, would revert to the CP.

The rights conferred in the secret agreement allowed WP principal McLaughlin to build his fortune. It later became a significant factor in the development of Livermore.

The act provided for bonds based on miles constructed as well as grants of public lands. The bonds and grants were added to enhance financial investment into the project. "Public lands" were specifically defined in the act as land "not sold, reserved or otherwise disposed of by the United States, and to which preemption or homestead claim may have not been registered by the time the line of said road was fixed." This provision supposedly protected the Spanish and Mexican land grants stated in the 1848 Treaty of Guadalupe Hidalgo which ended the Mexican-American War.[17]

Huntington, based in New York to raise funds for the CP, learned the ways of the unscrupulous stock swindlers, namely Cornelius Vanderbilt, Jay Gould, Daniel Drew, Jim Fisk, and others. He assimilated their techniques to manipulate railroad stocks to prevent competition, build a CP monopoly, and own his fortune.

Construction of the Pacific Railroad could not begin until after the Civil War when materials and manpower became available. Judah was dissatisfied with the nonexistent construction of what he called "my little road." Huntington, angry with Judah for not recommending him for president of the corporation, cut Judah out of his communiques. Judah felt that he was being treated as if he were not a member of the board even though he was still chief engineer. He headed back to New York, seeking investors who could give him control of the company. A week after arriving in New York, he died of yellow fever contracted while crossing Panama.

To sweeten the pot for the railroads, the 1864 amendment to the Pacific Railway Act redefined the terms of the government bonds and the land grants to alternate sections for 10 miles on either side of the 400-foot-wide right-of-way. The bonds were to be issued for each 20 miles completed.[18]

The WP charter was recognized and included into the Pacific Railway Act by Congress and the president in the 1865 amendment. The amendment added the WP line as the final leg of the railroad connecting to San Francisco. It brought into force Huntington's secret assignment of rights with the SF&SJ principals. The terms of the WP agreement were only published in the newspapers nearly a year after they were formalized. The amendment included the same terms for the WP as granted in the original bill, including the bonds and land grants.

The principal WP partners were Judge Timothy Dame, president and principal manager, Donahue, Houston, and McLaughlin.[19] The firm of McLaughlin and Houston was hired for the construction. Eventually, McLaughlin and Houston parted ways, leaving the construction firm entirely to McLaughlin. Public sparring among the San Francisco railroad investors, Judge Dame, and Governor Stanford continued over the Western terminus of the Pacific Railroad, despite the secret agreement.[20]

The goal of each of the three companies chartered to build the railroad was to use federal and other people's money. Each of the companies organized separate corporations for the actual construction and banking. This was done to hide the finances from the government and the stockholders of the parent companies. The construction corporations were owned by the principals of the railroad companies but not their general stock and bondholders. By keeping actual construction costs well below the contracted rates, they fraudulently created huge profits that went directly into the pockets of the principals. The Associates incorporated the Contract and Finance Company, with Charles Crocker as its president. Similarly, the Union Pacific established the Crédit Mobilier Company and the WP incorporated Charles McLaughlin Co.[21]

The companies also sought local jurisdictions to offer and guarantee bonds, which were sold to provide cash supporting the construction.[22] Special deals with supposed considerable profit potential were also sold or given to "friends" of the railroad. These friends were financiers and politicians. "Competitors" became friends when deals were made. When times were tough, bonds and stocks were often discounted, and friendly special deals often came to naught. This was true for the WP, CP, and UP. The big difference between the railroads was that UP President Thomas Durant was more public about his dealings, whereas Huntington and McLaughlin kept them secret.

McLaughlin subcontracted the actual construction of the WP to his own corporation and hired war hero Jerome B. Cox, with his firms of Cox and Arnold (later Cox and Meyers) for the initial construction from San Jose to Livermore Pass.[23]

Chinese labor was used in the construction of the Sacramento Valley Railroad, the first railroad in California.[24] McLaughlin hired Chinese in the construction of the SF&SJ and continued doing so for the WP, well before the practice was adopted by the CP. James Harvey Strobridge, the CP superintendent, was adamantly opposed to hiring Chinese laborers. Crocker ordered him to try the Chinese when he could not hire more than 800 white laborers. Many Chinese who had arrived during the gold rush were not welcomed into the Civil War armies, local society, or employment, even when white labor was scarce.[25] The Chinese workers became the real builders of both the WP and CP.

Surveys and infrastructure advanced well ahead of actual track laying. Initial construction of the WP was well done and much remains in service to this day.

McLaughlin apparently did not comprehend the considerable increase in cost and complexity of building in Alameda Cañón compared with the SF&SJ on flat land beside the bay. Much was spent on the construction of retaining walls, three major bridges, and significant cuts and fills within the canyon. He ran out of funds but pushed track laying to the 20-mile point so that the federal bonds could be collected.

The federal inspection train on October 2, 1866, was a gala event attended by the principals of the railroad and their friends. After the inspection train, the WP was issued its first land grants and government bonds.[26] The event was memorialized by the San Jose photographer John H. Heering. The end point of the first 20 miles was on a big curve in Alameda Canõn. That curve was supposed to be bypassed by a tunnel, and the track was built as a temporary runaround. The tunnel was never built, and the runaround track became permanent. Today, the buttressed masonry wall seen in Heering's photo is still doing its job. Part of the wall remains visible where it was not later buried under rocks and dirt from nearby landslides.

With the daunting costs for additional bridges and a tunnel, further WP construction was halted. He was significantly over budget and in breach of his contract with the WP and its secret agreement with the CP. Subcontractor Cox was not reimbursed for the $50,000 of his own money spent on the initial 20-mile construction. The contracted Chinese construction workers were also not paid. McLaughlin was already involved in legal disputes regarding his contracts both with the WP principals and his subcontractors. He wished to be relieved of his WP contract. Judge Edwin Crocker, Charles Crocker's brother, had long wanted the CP to get the charter for the Sacramento to San Francisco leg of the project. Cash was tight as the CP priority was the building across

The federal inspection train and end of first 20 miles celebration occurred October 2, 1866. (*Randy Hees, Ardenwood Historic Farm*)

the Sierra. Judge Crocker learned of McLaughlin's issues and felt he could force an inexpensive acquisition of the WP. Negotiations between McLaughlin, CP's Judge Crocker and WP's Judge Dame concluded with a CP takeover of the WP. McLaughlin was relieved of his commitments but personally retained the land grants. His grants were thought to have little value because of the preponderance of Mexican land grants supposedly protected by the Treaty of Guadalupe Hidalgo. Remaining WP rights of future bonds were assigned to the Contract & Finance Company.[27]

With the WP takeover, the Associates redefined the interpretation of "east from Pacific tidal waters" and shifted interest of the western terminus to the Oakland waterfront or possibly Goat Island (now Yerba Buena Island). A ferry across the Bay from Oakland to San Francisco would be a significantly shorter route than via San Jose to San Francisco. The San Francisco and Oakland railroad interests continued to disagree over where the terminus of the Pacific Railroad should be. They were unaware that the decision had been made for them.[28]

With no construction for more than six months, the press and public were unaware of the CP takeover. The press were beginning to question the future of the WP and the value of its bonds. *The Stockton Independent* noted:

> … San Joaquin County subscribed and issued $250,000 in bonds to aid the construction of the Western Pacific Railroad. Of course, no one can be silly enough to suppose that these bonds will ever be paid unless the consideration for which they were issued is received. If the road is not built the bonds will not be paid—at least that is our candid opinion. There is bad faith somewhere in this business, and the people of this region will not accept promises in lieu of performance any longer. There has been too much time lost already in financiering instead of building the road. When the work is under way we shall begin to think the road is to be built. We care not who builds it.[29]

In the same article, it was noted that the president of the WP earlier had promised completion of the Sacramento to Stockton portion within ninety days. Stockton had considerably longer than ninety days to wait. It was subsequently rumored that the CP was about to get control of the WP.

Notices of lawsuits by defrauded railroad stockholders were appearing in the press at about the same time. Their claims included that their stock was being procured by the directors without valuable consideration and that the directors were enriching themselves by defrauding the ordinary stockholders. Little became of such suits as, by then, Stanford had promoted the railroad's friends to the highest levels of the state government and courts. Lawsuits for non-payment of bills or stock manipulation were noticed in the press, including Cox's suit against the WP and McLaughlin for non-payment of his construction expenses of the first 20 miles was on the Supreme Court docket.

Leland Stanford became president of the newly acquired WP. Euphemistically, the WP line became known as the "Governor's Road."[30] The takeover helped quell the intercity rivalry between San Francisco and Sacramento regarding where the western end of the Pacific Railway would be. Huntington was not happy with the deal as it stoked disagreements within the Associates. It considerably increased his enmity with Stanford for acting without him and not being named president in the first place. Both the terms of the WP deal and the squabbles of the Associates were kept secret from the press. The WP and CP companies were not officially merged until the year after the completion of the railroads.[31] The WP was initially operated and identified as a separate company for some time after the merger.

From his position in New York, Huntington was aware of and trying to head off competition on the horizon. He encouraged the Associates, led by Stanford and Judge Crocker, to acquire significant other holdings. The term "the Associates" is used for these transactions because they were agreed to by the individuals involved and not necessarily by the stockholders. The acquisitions were later revealed in the press and called swindles. Stanford immediately responded that such rumors were "without foundation."[32]

The financial difficulties of the WP stockholders also placed other SF&SJ holdings in jeopardy. President Johnson had signed a bill, awarding land grants but not bonds to three unbuilt but potential competitors: the Atlantic & Pacific, the California & Oregon, and the SF&SJ's Southern Pacific (SP).[33] Southern Pacific and also the California & Oregon were subsequently folded into the Associates' holdings. The important acquisitions also included the SF&SJ, which gave the Associates uncontested access to San Francisco.

The California Pacific Railroad (Cal-P) was chartered by a competitive group of San Francisco investors, to build from Sacramento to Vallejo along the northern side of the Carquinez Strait. Their plan was to bypass the WP line with a ferry to San Francisco, which would be both faster and cheaper to operate. Huntington acquired the Cal-P with an under the table payment to its president.[34]

The Associates cultivated power and fortune by providing favors for their friends and expecting favors and loyalty in return. The favors included valuable stock options, loans, free transit passes on railroads, seats on boards of directors, and favorable court rulings. The complexity of the organizations with their various friends and stockholders caused some deals not to be completed for years. The WP and CP companies were not officially merged until June 23, 1870.[35] The formal merger of the CP into the SP did not occur for more than seventy years.

Thomas Durant, the flamboyant head of the UP, was just as corrupt as Huntington. Crédit Mobilier was the construction and money laundering arm of the UP principals, similar to the Contract & Finance Company. After the railroad was completed, a suit of UP stockholders opened the unsavory details of stocks being handed out or sold at advantageous prices to politicians. A congressional investigation, known as the Crédit Mobilier Scandal, was launched, and U.S. Marshals seized the UP's books in 1873.[36] The vice president, speaker of the house, and several senators and congressmen were implicated in the scheme. Representative Oaks Ames was censured for helping distribute the stock. The rest were conveniently forgotten in the election year.

Huntington's hermit-like existence and secretive dealings kept him out of the limelight for a while. He realized the Associates' jeopardy, especially after obfuscating as a witness before Congress. He had the Associates quickly disband the Contract and Finance Company.[37] Details of the multitude of the Associates' agreements were not revealed publicly. Many were lost when Contract and Finance Company records were intentionally burned before federal agents arrived during the scandal in July 1873. The Western Development Company was formed and owned by the Associates to carry on the business.[38]

A Scottish surveyor named Arthur Keddie was exploring the old Indian trails up the Feather River for a potential wagon road before Donner Pass was completed. He found that a route suitable for a railroad could be built to transverse the Sierra over Beckwourth Pass. He noted that the pass was more than 2,000 feet lower than Donner Pass and felt it would be a superior railroad route, especially in the winter. The Oroville and Virginia City Railroad Company (O&VC) was formed by Keddie and several important businessmen.

Dodge was asked to consider approaching the government to fund Keddie's route. Keddie started construction east of Oroville while trying to convince Congress to support the project. Congress refused Keddie's proposal as they were not willing to support a second route even when the first was not finished. Keddie was dismissed by Huntington for a request for support since Donner Pass had just been completed, and they were racing the UP to build across Nevada and Utah. The O&VC died along with Keddie's project for lack of funds. Years later, Keddie's survey was adopted by Jay and George Gould to compete with the CP.[39]

When the Donner Summit Tunnel was completed, Crocker was able to release teams of mostly Chinese workers and restart construction on the

WP line. In mid-March 1868, 250 laborers were reported grading from Sacramento towards Stockton. Two major time-consuming obstacles remained for the WP: the bridge over the San Joaquin River and the Livermore Pass with its summit tunnel. At the same time, it was reported that contracts were let for the western portion of the WP line.[40] They detached many of their men from the west of Livermore Pass and set them constructing east from the WP's 20-mile point completed by the former owners of the franchise. They worked up Alameda Cañon into the Livermore Valley. They had about 2,000 men at work and claimed the railroad would be completed by the following August.[41]

Work on the Livermore Pass Summit Tunnel progressed rapidly in early February, with a working force of about 400 persons, mostly Chinese. One hundred horses, dump carts, and harnesses, which had been used in grading the CP line, arrived in Sacramento. They were sent overland to their destination via Stockton. Horses and carts were also sent by schooner, with a large quantity of powder, to Mohr's Landing and then taken to the tunnel by cart. Various small delays were constantly reported. *The Sacramento Daily Union* reported:

> Two or three hundred of the graders who lately arrived from the railroad front have been engaged to work on the Western Pacific Railroad. The steamer, *Goodman Castle*, was to take them over to Shepherd's Ferry yesterday, but when the time came for the *Castle* to leave, a large number of the men failed to put in an appearance, having found it impossible to forsake the pleasures of the city so soon after their long exile on the plains. The steamer leaves for Shepherd's Ferry this morning, towing the barge *San Antonio* loaded with cobbles for the bridge to be constructed at that point. Many of the laborers will take passage by her for the scene of their future operations.[42]

Work on the Livermore Pass Summit Tunnel had been temporarily suspended on account of a scarcity of timber.[43] A severe earthquake was felt at both Stockton and the tunnel. The men working in the tunnel were said to have made very quick time in getting to the open air.[44] On another day, a locomotive sent out to aid ballasting the track was returned to Sacramento because excessive sparks were setting fires in the grain fields along the road.[45] The tunnel was holed through with daylight visible in mid-August. The track was expected to be laid in about ten days hence.[46] The track eastward from Vallejo Mills was finished to Laddsville on the same day. The Livermore Summit Tunnel, at 1,200 feet, was the second in length on the entire CP line, only exceeded by the Donner Summit Tunnel. On the next day, track was laid to within a mile of Shepherd's Ferry on the

San Joaquin River. Farmers on the west side of the San Joaquin River and in the Livermore Valley raised large quantities of grain awaiting shipment by rail. On the same day, 1,029 tons of wheat were shipped from Stockton.[47] The railroad was pushing to have direct transportation available from San Francisco and San Jose to Sacramento for the September 7 opening of the California State Fair. The San Francisco Bay Railroad, owned by the Associates, was only completed between Vallejo's Mill and San Lorenzo.[48] Temporary arrangements were made with Alameda Railroad and Ferry Company to ferry people from San Francisco to the Alameda wharf and share trackage to San Lorenzo. On September 6, 1869, the bridge across the San Joaquin River was finished and three trains crossed it, one for San Jose and two for Alameda.[49] Regular service of two trains a day in each direction commenced the next day to and from Sacramento, and connecting service between San Francisco and San Jose. A correspondent for the *Daily Alta California* penned the account of the entrance of the first train into Alameda:

> The opening of the Western Pacific Railroad from Stockton to Alameda was finally consummated last evening by the arrival at the latter place of the first through train. Hereafter the trains will leave twice daily: passengers leave San Francisco by the Alameda Ferry, at 7 a.m. and 3:30 p.m.

On the days following the first trains, the major Bay Area newspapers carried two advertisements. A special $3 round-trip excursion fare to Sacramento for the state fair was announced. For passengers from San Francisco, the ferry and passage over the San Francisco & Alameda Railroad was included in the fare. Rail service to the Oakland ferry and the waterfront, now firmly in the control of the Associates, was initiated two months later.[50] The connection to Oakland completed the western portion of the federal Pacific Railway project. The final task of the project was the construction of the Missouri River bridge from Council Bluffs Iowa to Omaha Nebraska completed in 1872.

The term "transcontinental railroad" is somewhat of a misnomer. It did not actually mean one railroad completely across the continent, but rather connections to navigable waterways of both the Atlantic and Pacific. It provided the quickest, safest, and most reliable route for both passengers and goods, although it involved several railroads and required multiple transfers from one service to another. If you bought a ticket for the entire trip, it was really a book of tickets for each of the railroads and ferries as well. Even though you could travel across the country mostly by rail for the first time, there were a couple of inconveniences along the way. From New York, the trip started with a ferry to New Jersey where the Pennsylvania Railroad would take travelers to Chicago. From there they would have to make their way across town to the Chicago & North Western, which would take them to Council Bluffs, Iowa. From there, passengers would take a ferry to Omaha, Nebraska, where the UP would travel to Promontory. There the CP would take over for the final leg to Oakland and another ferry to San Francisco. The train route from Chicago to Oakland became known as the Overland route, and the first-class through trains were named the Overland Limited.

The Associates had no interest in and were totally inept at running a railroad. Years later, Charles Crocker was quoted telling Governor Fredrick Low, "We built the road for the profits we could make in building it, and when we got it done, we didn't know what the devil to do with it."[51]

3

TOWN EMERGES

The Livermore Valley changed completely from frontier cattle ranching to a prosperous farming community. Several ranches were established in the valley and the surrounding hills by an influx of settlers from the East. Many with farming experience came after unsuccessfully having sought riches in the gold rush.

The railroad precipitated the founding and growth of the town of Livermore, which became the major support for the valley. Isolated ranches became part of a close-knit community. The ways of doing business, communication, and the cultural environment evolved with the town. The railroad allowed the profitable shipment of produce to markets and the import of necessary goods.

A squatter, Alphonso "Frank" Ladd, in 1864, preempted a quarter section carved from Las Positas after the death of Livermore. He initially built a hotel with a saloon. That attracted a small settlement at the junction of trails from the Bay Area to the Central Valley. The settlement became known as Laddsville and was the only population center at the eastern end of the Livermore valley before the coming of the railroad.[1] Laddsville had a population of about fifty people in 1868, many of whom later moved to Livermore. Alexander Mesa built a saloon in late 1864, which was deemed, "more necessary than a church or school."[2] The first general store was started by Henry Goetjen that winter. A hotel with an Italian restaurant was built by Anton Bardellini. Israel Horton and Andrew J. McLeod built houses exclusively as residences. Merchants often lived in their business establishment instead of an exclusive residence. Settlers were mostly self-sufficient for their foods, by raising their own or trading locally. General stores' main business was providing all the necessities for frontier living that included kitchen supplies, dry goods, clothing, farm tools, guns, ammunition, etc.

Structures in Laddsville were initially quickly and poorly built as most materials were brought in by wagon. Some were built or rebuilt after the railroad came through. Laddsville was a typical frontier settlement and considered a "lively town."[3] It was said to be a slow day when only three fights broke out. Shootings and robberies were commonplace.[4] Desperados, cattle rustlers, and prospectors were regular customers at Ladd's Hotel and Saloon. Ladd refused another drink demanded by a desperado named Hyde, who was already drunk. Hyde threw a water pitcher and then a beer jug at Ladd. They scuffled to the floor, and a shot went off killing Hyde with his own gun. Ladd was not charged on the basis of self-defense.[5] There were many murders and assaults in and around Laddsville and later in Livermore.[6]

A drugstore run by Doctors Knight and Sproule provided minimal medical services. It was suggested a "pest house" be established after several smallpox deaths.[7] A fire destroyed much of Laddsville on the morning of September 26, 1871. Apparently, the fire broke out in the Knight & Sproul drugstore, where Dr. Knight was struck in the forehead by an exploding cartridge. Bardellini's Washington Hotel, B. Meyer & Co., Goetjen's general merchandise and post office, A. J. Alores barber shop, in addition to the drugstore, were all lost.[8] The Laddsville Saloon later burned to the ground. It was a landmark from before Livermore was platted.[9]

A post office in Laddsville was opened by Goetjen and called Nottingham not Laddsville.[10] Apparently, Nottingham was the name Livermore had given to his nearby homestead in recognition of his origin. Then in July 1870, the post office name was changed to Livermore, though both Nottingham and Laddsville names were still recognized by the postal service. After Frank Ladd died "of whisky" in 1868, his wife, Sarah, continued to manage the hotel and saloon.

A drought in 1864 caused William Mendenhall significant losses while living in the Sycamore Valley.[11] Mendenhall returned to Santa Clara, where he continued raising fine racehorses.

The Bernal's Rancho El Valle de San José was also suffering financial difficulty. Family feuding over inheritance issues and drought forced it into bankruptcy. The *rancho* was formally surveyed, subdivided into sixty-four plots, and given to Hill and Harmon Land Agents for sale in 1864. Mendenhall had other interests and land holdings in the valley, even though he was living in Santa Clara. The Mendenhall brothers (William, Martin, and Absalom) maintained either together or individually purchased several Bernal plots.[12]

The Western Pacific Railroad (WP) was initially created and run by local businessmen with whom Mendenhall had likely become acquainted.

The railroad published the survey map of its route from San José to Sacramento in 1875. The map is large, quite detailed, and accurate. It specifically showed Livermore's house and Ladd's 1864 hotel, also several Bernal houses in the western part of the valley. The map also named the Livermore Pass and Livermore Plain, showing all the trails into and out of the valley.

Mendenhall had apparently seen the railroad's survey through the valley. It is likely to have sparked Mendenhall's interest in the Bernal's bankruptcy plot No. 18. The plot was crossed by the WP's surveyed right-of-way and was bounded to the east by Rancho Las Positas. Mendenhall and the railroad recognized that a new town, serving the ranching and farming community, would grow up around a station and bring business to the railroad. The railroad also recognized that location would be a site for an additional locomotive to help trains to climb over Livermore Pass. Mendenhall was also aware of the policy that if you wanted a station at a given site you had to give the railroad the property.

Bernal plot No. 18 was initially purchased by George Curtner for $10,000. William Mendenhall with brother Martin purchased the plot from Curtner for $11,900. It is likely that William agreed to give a station site to the railroad with a handshake long before his purchase was finalized. He subsequently cleared the title to the plot, entirely in his name just a few weeks before the completion of the railroad. The station site was named Livermore before the deed was given to the WP, demonstrating the commitment for the site had been made earlier.

William Mendenhall filed a plat for a town just weeks after the railroad went into service. Handwriting in the lower right copy of the plat is by Alameda County's deputy recorder. It certifies the plat was recorded November 4, 1869, at 3:40 p.m., at the request of William M. Mendenhall.

Mendenhall named the town Livermore for the deceased valley pioneer. Laddsville was the only settlement in the valley, and a plat for the new town was of minor general interest. The plat filing was a momentous occasion for the valley, even though the notice in the *San Jose Mercury-News* was just two sentences on a back page, "The new town of Livermore, about one third of a mile from Laddsville, has been laid out by W. M. Mendenhall. The town is in Alameda County, on the line of the Western Pacific Railway."[13]

The plat covered 680 acres and was entirely within the surveyed Bernal plot No. 18. There was no development and no one living there at the time. Later the *San Jose Mercury* declared: "Laddsville was the oldest and less improved of any place in the valley."[14]

The design of Mendenhall's plat was clearly for the railroad to support the town and the town to provide business for the railroad. The

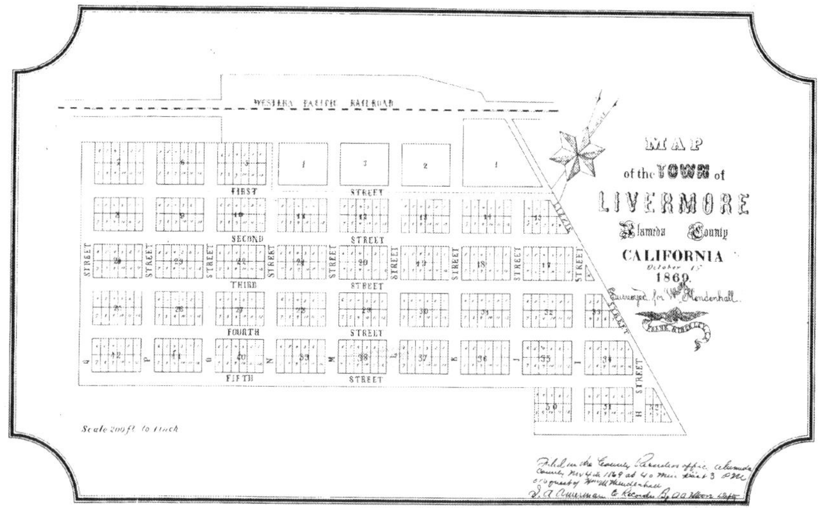

Plat for the town of Livermore. The handwriting in the lower right is the registrar's acknowledgement of the date and time of the filing. (*Livermore Heritage Guild*)

arrangement of commercial blocks one through four were set back from the existing track to create the station space. In the plat, the railroad was indicated by just a dotted line across the top. The plat contained forty-four lots between today's First and Fifth Streets and from Lizzie Street to Q Street.

Lizzie Street was named after Mendenhall's daughter, Sarah Elizabeth, and ran along the border between the Bernal plot and Rancho Las Positas. Lizzie Street was eventually renamed South Livermore Avenue. Space was reserved for a park, two churches, and a school. Livermore rapidly became the economic and cultural center for the valley.

Laddsville was not a legal entity and therefore was never formally incorporated into Livermore. After the many fires, some structures remained or were rebuilt. It was likely included into Livermore when the city limits were extended in the mid-twentieth century.

A cluster of adobes west of what became Laddsville was called Little Mexico. It was thought to originally house the Spanish-speaking native and Mexican workers of Rancho Las Positas. Little Mexico became known for its dancing girls and bordello after Livermore was established. The county eventually refused to issue retail liquor licenses for establishments in the area.

Bullfights as well were conducted in a small ring between Laddsville and Little Mexico until 1874. The ring was about 30 feet in diameter with a 7-foot fence surrounded by several rows of benches. There were also bear *versus* bull fights, though local bears were eventually killed off by the ranchers. The famous bear trainer and circus performer Grizzly Adams captured his bears around the valley two decades earlier.[15]

Geologist Joseph LeConte camped overnight in Laddsville just after Livermore was platted. He disagreed with population figures of 200 citizens at the time. He claimed: "one hundred and fifty of them were dogs who barked all night."[16]

The railroad created the ability of shipping of large volume and weight farm products and materials to growing markets across the hills to both the Bay Area and California's Central Valley. Virtually everything necessary for the town and shipment of products to markets began to come and go via the railroad. Ranchers in the valley reconsidered the ways to profit from the land.

Travel time from Livermore to Oakland was reduced from two or more days to about two hours. Passengers could now make a round trip and conduct some business in a single day, although it was never convenient for regular commuters.

An early timetable published one month after the completion of the railroad shows two passenger trains each way stopping in Livermore. The timetable also showed two scheduled freight trains daily in each direction.[17] Additional freight trains were necessary at harvest times to export the large volume of grains.

Stations in the earliest timetable give some historical context to the region. Livermore was the only station listed in the valley. Pleasanton was part of the remaining Bernal *ranchero* and not yet a town. Laddsville was not listed despite the fact it was populated before anyone lived in Livermore. Neither Niles nor Tracy had yet been established.

Instead, San Jose Junction and Bantas were listed. Bantas was a landing on the San Joaquin River. San Jose Junction was a temporary location in Alameda Canõn where the rail lines from San Jose and Oakland met.

The gift deed from Mendenhall to the WP was filed in the spring of 1870, following the beginning of railroad service. The WP was still a separate corporation until the formal merger in the summer of 1870, although it was actually owned and operated by the CP since McLaughlin's failure in 1866. The gift deed was not recorded for about six months after the plat, likely because of negotiations for small-parcel adjustments and a detailed survey. The changes indicate that Mendenhall was likely consulting on its design with an executive of the railroad. The small adjustments from parcels adjoining a proposed downtown rail loop siding were added to the gift to the WP.[18] Those plots rapidly became committed to businesses owners moving from Laddsville to Livermore for direct access to the railroad. They included C. J. Stevens, C. J. Bond, McLeod, H. Meyers, G.

Forbes, J. Wilkinson, J. Beazell, S. Welteran, O. B. Stillwell, H. Cromwell, and M. Durand.[19]

Through the years, the amount of property Mendenhall granted to the WP has been quoted as varying from 10 to 32 acres. The size of the grant is more generally thought to have been 20 acres. The confusion in the size of Mendenhall's grant may arise from three different statements in Wood's *History of Alameda County*.[20] The adjustments of the business owners' plots may also have added to the confusion. The Ladd family, without a deed, were not able to offer any property to the railroad. As a result, the village lost out on a very lucrative opportunity and its future viability.

Laddsville remained small and was eventually annexed into Livermore. It continued to be identified as a neighborhood by its proud citizens.

The railroad initiated a change of the valley's economy from its ranching origins to more valuable agriculture. Before the railroad ranchers planted enough grains to support their herds in difficult times. Wagons could not carry profitable amounts of grain across the hills to markets. Moving large numbers of cattle and sheep to market was also not profitable; however, their byproducts, hides, tallow, wool, etc. provided sufficient trade and income. The railroad provided a cost-effective way for bulk shipment to market. Landowners rapidly shifted from ranchers to grain farmers. They were able to plant as much grains as their land would support, which exceeded the value of their cattle ranching. In the spring before the completion of the railroad, a correspondent of the *Alameda Democrat* reported that twice as many acres of wheat were being planted in the Livermore Valley.[21]

Mendenhall gave Calvin J. Stevens the 5-acre lot No. 1 of the plat on the condition he build a flour mill. It was reported in the *San Jose Mercury-News* that the flour mill was burned in 1882 and not rebuilt.

The Livermore lodge of the Independent Order of Odd Fellows was formed in 1872 to help support the growth of new nonprofit associations. The two-story IOOF Hall was completed in 1874, and it is considered the second-oldest building in town that is still standing.

The oldest building in Livermore is not clear. Likely it is the mill itself, although the title is also claimed by owners of a private house.

Major fires in Laddsville in 1871 and 1874 decimated the village. Most burned-out Laddsville businesses were insured and rebuilt in Livermore. They included the Knight & Sproul drugstore and Bardellini's Washington Hotel. Bardellini built a new, larger hotel on the southeast corner of First and L streets in Livermore, opening in 1875.[22] The lots along the station site were quickly bought by former Laddsville businessmen.

Stevens and Wilkinson also built a block-long grain and hay warehouse adjacent to the siding in downtown. Part of that track was on property

Overview of Calvin Stevens' lot in the town. Stevens' flour mill has the smoking chimney on the right. Behind the flour mill along the railroad is the Stevens and Wilkinson's grain warehouse. The Magnolia Saloon is center left. The Independent Order of Odd Fellows' hall is the two-story building on the far left and still stands today. (*New Historical Atlas of Alameda County, Thompson & West, 1878*)

Stevens donated to the railroad and was situated so that rail cars could be directly loaded from the warehouse. Stevens became Livermore's second mayor after the town was incorporated six years later and was twice again elected mayor.

The Station's Agency was established with the completion of the railroad. John L. Mitchel was appointed its first agent and served until he retired from the railroad more than thirty years later.

Mitchel was responsible for the major business functions of the station, including ticketing of passengers, weighing, billing, and routing of the freight. He was the chief telegrapher, receiving orders and information on train movements from dispatchers, and he set the train-order semaphore to signal an engineer to slow or stop for orders. Part of his agents' duties included representing Wells Fargo's express service as well as the Western Union Telegraph Company.

Railroad business in Livermore was initially conducted from a boxcar until the first depots were completed in 1870.[23] The separate freight and passenger depots were built in the middle of the station site, on either

John L. Mitchel, *circa* 1883. (*M. W.
Wood, History of Alameda County*)

side of L Street. The original passenger depot was a very small structure, indicating that not much passenger traffic was expected. Mitchel recognized that the welfare of the town was good business for the railroad and personally took responsibility for both. He built a house and lived at L and Third streets.

He was elected to the town Board of Trustees the year following his becoming station agent and was reelected every year until retiring from the board in 1900. In addition to his railroad job, he served as secretary of the Farmers' Union. From his office at the depot, he was also an independent insurance agent, salesman of farm machinery, and the town's ice distributor.[24] He delivered 10,000 pounds of ice to the town in one month at three cents a pound.[25] Mitchel reported the many carloads of grains, cattle, wine, bricks, minerals from the mines, gold, silver, cash, and business records were shipped each week.

The depot became the area's early meeting place for the latest information and gossip. It was kept open throughout the night for major national election returns.[26]

Mitchel recorded and provided weather information to farmers a full twenty years before the establishment of the National Weather Service.

Mitchel was the railroad's local employment agent. He was the railroad's interface with the town and had the rule of law for any interaction with the railroad. Those interested in long-term employment by the railroad had to be proficient telegraphers.

Their assignments as regular employees were long-term, often for a lifetime. Young apprentices were hired as roustabouts. Their job was to find and wake overnighting train crew members when called to duty, often in the middle of the night. To find those crew members, they had to know every flophouse in the area. They usually bunked in the passenger depot and helped load and unload the freight. Others were hired as needed to help with the freight.

The earliest track plan for the Livermore station was designed to take full advantage of Mendenhall's gift and plat.[27] The plan was drawn by the Western Pacific Railroad in 1869 in a book with all their station plans. The Livermore station ran from east of Maple Street to west of what became S Street. It was much wider than the standard 400-foot railroad right of way, from just north of the First Street blocks of town to beyond the future Railroad Avenue.

The original separate freight and passenger depots are shown on either side of what became L Street. The passenger depot is located directly alongside the main through track with a platform extending across the future L Street. The tracks include a passing siding on the north side of the main track. A siding to serve the downtown businesses along the southern edge of the station property. A siding called the "house track" serving the freight depot was south of the depots, between the mainline and the downtown siding. A turntable and engine house were on a short spur split from the western end of the house track.

The passing and downtown sidings connected with the main line at Maple Street and at P Street. The shorter house track split from the main line at Lizzie Street and rejoined the main near P street. The track plan did not change for about twenty years, though the drawing was occasionally modified to show the businesses being served.

Barely a month after the filing of the town plat, a San Francisco reporter was amazed by the area's metamorphosis from a wild and unsettled country to a busy, flourishing agricultural town. He noted that this change was due to the ranchers' ability to grow large amounts of hay and grain then transport it to market by rail rather than hauling it in wagons across the hills.[28] Bringing cattle to market was hardly mentioned in the press, as cattle were historically driven to markets or processed to hides and tallow before leaving the ranch. The rapid development of the town was aided by rail delivery of building materials.

Twenty-eight buildings were erected the year after the plat filing and more were under construction.[29] Commercial development was concentrated along First Street and included hotels, all sorts of small shops, and multiple saloons.

James Beazell and his brother, Albert, built the earliest blacksmith shop in Livermore. It was situated alongside the downtown siding adjacent to Stevens' warehouse. Beazell later became a state senator who introduced the bill to incorporate the town of Livermore.

The ranches in Livermore Valley and surrounding hills were relatively far apart and individual one-room schoolhouses were built to accommodate the children. Public subscriptions were required to build and operate these schools. These schools generally had one teacher for the first through eighth grades. Most of these were declared school districts, registered in the county, with two person boards of directors.

There was some state support for these schools as long as they had a minimum of fifteen students. Schools with fewer students were deemed "lapsed" and dropped from district designation, losing state funding. The school district (identified later as the Livermore Elementary School District) was formed in 1862, seven years before the town was platted.[30] The district included the eastern portion of the valley and surrounding hills and annexed many of the one-room districts and "lapsed" schools.

The one-room school that first served near to Robert Livermore Junior's house was built by Israel Horton in late 1866. Horton's school became the first school in the plated town after it was moved to McLeod's property on Maple Street. Mendenhall gave the school district a block on Fifth between I and J Streets. The Horton school house was later moved there. Most of the one-room schools were abandoned or demolished. The May School building survived for more than 100 years until it was destroyed by an arson fire in 1979.

The town passed a supporting tax to construct a public grammar school. The school was completed on the Fifth Street site in 1877 and was within walking distance of most Livermore residents at the time.

Grammar school on Fifth Street, built in 1877. (*Livermore Heritage Guild*)

Livermore Collegiate Institute. (*Livermore Heritage Guild*)

The Livermore Collegiate Institute was founded by Reverend and Mrs. W. B. Kingsbury on land donated by Mendenhall in the first year after the filing of the plat. The college was located just south of Mendenhall's plat on what became College Avenue.

The public schools only taught the lower grades. The college was called a school of higher learning, but in reality, it was closer to being a high school. It was financed by tuition and included some students' room and board. The school rapidly grew with students coming from nearby settlements. An initial three-story building was constructed with financial aid from Mendenhall. It outgrew its initial building two years before the incorporation of Livermore. The Kingsburys could not afford the necessary expansion and sold the school to James Dale Smith. Smith was a professor at Washington College in Irvington.

The college was instrumental in raising the town's appreciation of the performing arts with many public performances of students and guest artists. They subsequently gave recitals and theatrical performances to appreciative audiences at the school's Washington Hall. Faculty members offered classes and private lessons in singing, piano, and the playing of other instruments.[31] They also started a dancing school.[32]

Washington Hall remained the town's main performance venue until the opening of the Farmers' Union Theater with 650 seats.[33] The 800-seat Sweeney Opera House became the major performance venue just after the turn of the century.[34] Fine arts were displayed at the post office, including a series of portraits of the town's leading men done by an artist from Oakland.[35]

Religious congregations began forming in the valley several years before the plat of the town. Itinerant preachers would occasionally pass through providing a sermon to a few settlers mostly in or around Laddsville. Catholic settlers built a small chapel built on the Ladd's property. However, they initially had to travel to Mission San Jose to attend mass. Saint Michael Catholic Mission was established in 1872. They did not have a regular priest for another six years. Rev. John F. Cassidy celebrated the first mass in 1878. Thirteen years later, in 1891, a church was built on property sold to the church for $1 by the Ladd family.

Rev. B. N. Seymour preached the first Presbyterian service in the valley in 1866 and a few times thereafter. Monthly Presbyterian services were started by Rev. William Wallace Brier the following May. The first services were conducted at Horton's School on what is now Portola Avenue.[36] Later that year, the Methodist lay pastor Theron H. Tooker hosted a small congregation at his home. The small Methodist congregation also included Episcopalians. The Methodists alternated services with the Presbyterians at the schoolhouse. The two congregations met at the Livermore Collegiate

St. Michael Catholic Church, built in Laddsville in 1891. (*Livermore Heritage Guild*)

Institute after it was formed. The congregations moved to the second floor of the Bank Exchange Hall because the college was too far out of town. They were upstairs from a saloon much to the displeasure of the women in the congregations.[37] Mendenhall donated lots for the Presbyterian and Methodist Episcopal churches at Forth and K streets gnd at Third and I streets respectively. The Presbyterians built their chapel in 1874 leaving the Methodists above the saloon. The Methodists then used Fire House Hall on Sundays until their church was built in 1882.[38] A separate Episcopal church was built in 1902 at 5th and J streets and closed in 1919 due to a lack of parishioners.

Dry-land farming was the practice in the valley before irrigation. That meant farmers seeded their fields in the winter then prayed for rain. After a successful crop in the first year, many were disappointed by a hot and dry 1870. The crop was reported as an overall failure, although there were some good fields of whcat.[39] One farmer was able to supply 2,000 sacks of new wheat.[40] In the following dry and cold winter, many cattle grazing in the hills perished.[41] By the following February, more rain had fallen in Livermore than in the entire previous season, assuring a bountiful crop.[42] Stevens' warehouse was nearly full, and more grain was coming.[43] That

First Presbyterian Church, built in 1874. (*Livermore Heritage Guild*)

Methodist Church, built in 1882. (*Livermore Heritage Guild*)

Episcopal Church, built in 1902, closed in 1919 due to a lack of parishioners. (*Livermore Heritage Guild*)

winter, 8,000 more acres of grain were planted.[44] Then, in June, it was reported that the yield would be much better than expected. By September, it was reported that nearly 7.5 million pounds of grain had been shipped by rail from Livermore. Irrigation required regular water from creeks, wells, storage tanks, and reservoirs; facilities that were not available at the time. There was not sufficient water as the creeks often went dry in the summer.

The large amounts of grains and hay being harvested required dry storage before they could be sold and transported. The amounts were larger than the railroad could transport at any one time.

The building of multiple warehouses made them the major financial businesses in the town. Three major warehouses were built along the north side of the tracks by Esdon and Waterman and their business was incorporated as the Livermore Warehouse Company.

The successful San Francisco merchant, Abram Anspacher purchased the corner property along the downtown rail siding at First and L streets. By the following January, his sons opened a general store and grain warehouse, which rapidly became a mainstay of the community. A few years later, they owned the entire block from L to M streets. They built another grain warehouse and opened a lumberyard on railroad property west of M Street between the downtown siding and the main line. The store closed before World War I, although the warehouse continued until the death of Abram's grandson, Philip.[45] The lumberyard was eventually taken over by the Diamond Match Company and remained on the site through the middle of the twentieth century.

The newspapers from nearby towns occasionally published one or two lines about Livermore on a back page. Different incidents were often reported in a common paragraph, often with errors. The *Stockton Independent* reported on a back page:

> The farmers of Livermore Valley are very busy harvesting and threshing. The crop will be six times greater than that of last year. A pet bear belonging to Doctors Knight and Sproule broke from its cage today and running through the streets causing great confusion but doing no damage further than upsetting Doctor Easton, injuring him internally. His bearship was captured near Featherville.[46]

Water was essential for fighting the innumerable fires which caused costly loss of property, injury and deaths. Oil lamps, candles, wood, or coal-burning stoves most often initiated the burning of the hastily built wooden structures. Water was also necessary for the community and steam locomotives. A water company was formed, supplying water from

 Frontier to City

A train in front of the first passenger depot and Anspacher's store and warehouse. Earliest known photograph of a train in Livermore, *circa* 1875. (*Livermore Heritage Guild*)

wells to both the town and railroad.[47] Initially individual wells were dug as needed. In most cases, the water was pumped by a windmill and stored in an elevated tank. There also was a community well with a hand pump on first street. A cistern was used to store water for firefighting.

However, the cistern was insufficient.[48] The Arroyo Mocho Water Company began drawing water from the arroyo in 1873. The company began laying pipe to serve the downtown. The company failed because of intermittent supply and the smell of sulfur in the water. The Livermore Spring Water Company was formed the following year. It drew water from the Arroyo Las Positas which was stored in tanks. The company acquired the Arroyo Mocho company and added its water into its system. They started installing pipelines to directly provide water to the town. The water was not the best in quality, leaving rings in bathtubs and even a snake.[49]

Business during that once-a-year trip to market had usually been conducted through trade and, only as necessary, gold on the barrelhead. With distant rail shipments or orders arranged by telegraph, the simple market deals no longer worked. Right from the start, railroad ticket fares on the WP/CP required payment in cash. Banks and banking procedures rapidly emerged to process transactions. Original Livermore banks were later merged into larger regional institutions. The Bank of Livermore later became the Farmers & Merchants National Bank. It eventually merged with the Bank of Italy which became the Bank of America. The First National Bank of Livermore merged with American Trust and was later incorporated into Wells Fargo Bank.

The *San Jose Mercury* noted the town was springing to life in 1872:

> Livermore boasts of five hotels, flour mill, two blacksmith shops, a machine shop, seven stores, a young ladies seminary, three livery stables, tailors, doctors, shoemakers, lawyers, loafers and whisky mills innumerable, three warehouses and a Catholic church.

Livermore still had its tough element, The *San Jose Mercury-News* also declared there was a desperate set in the Livermore Valley.[50] A suspected murderer from Napa was captured nearby. He was handcuffed and transported to the nearest jail in San Leandro.[51] A nephew of Joaquin Murrieta, accused of multiple murders, was captured. Murrieta was one of the state's most wanted bandits. He had hidden in the hills between Livermore and Corral Hollow with his band of desperados.[52] The body of a man was found hanging from a tree at Oak Knoll trestle, adjacent to today's Murrieta Boulevard. The east-bound Overland train stopped to cut the man down.[53] A prize-fight, with a $200 purse, was arranged between James Mitchell of Livermore and Frank Smith of Napa.[54]

Six months before completion of the railroad, 640 acres of wheat land near Livermore's Pass was advertised for sale at $10 an acre.[55] Three months later, it was reported that the WP was paying $150 an acre.[56] $1.25 was the homesteader's cost for federal land. It appears that McLaughlin was trying to drive up the property value of his adjacent grant lands.

He retained ownership of the WP land grants after the CP takeover. McLaughlin, typical of the wheeler-dealer tycoons of the era, probably lost much of an earlier fortune in his WP debacle. McLaughlin claimed the Rancho Las Positas and other Mexican Land Grant Diseños were not proper surveys and therefore were invalid. The commissioner of the Land Office later upheld his claims.[57] The land office ruling was later upheld by the secretary of the interior and the Supreme Court of the United States. His land claims of alternate square-mile sections disenfranchised several early ranchers who did not have recorded deeds dated before the federal amendment of the Pacific Railroad Act of 1862, which recognized the WP. The rulings made him the second-largest landholder in California after Leland Stanford. However, his disenfranchisement of the early settlers made him one of the most hated people in the state. Livermore's properties were willed to his children and were mostly surveyed before the 1865 deadline. Robert Livermore Junior's farm was on the property willed to him by his father. His homestead was east of and close to his father's adobe along Las Positas creek. However, most of the remainder of the *ranchero* loosely described in Livermore's Mexican grant was not formally surveyed, thus claimed by McLaughlin.

The Bernals' Rancho El Valle de San José had been formally surveyed in the bankruptcy proceedings and was consequently not subject to McLaughlin's claims. The commissioner also validated some of the Ladd claim, allowing Sarah Ladd the 160-acre quarter section containing Laddsville.[58]

Mclaughlin began to quickly sell his sections once the commissioner was finally able to issue patents, that is clear titles for his claims. He claimed that the land was being sold by the railroad, even though he was the one selling it. He had an arrangement with William "Boss Billy" Carr, Stanford's political fixer, to market his properties in Alameda County.

McLaughlin demanded $30 to $40 per acre, considerably higher than the government homesteader's rate.[59] Good farming land and railroad access created a boom around Livermore despite the high prices. The land boom quickly rebuilt McLaughlin's fortune. His land was sold in 640-acre, square-mile sections. Sections were also being subdivided into 160-acre plots. The plots sold were much smaller than the thousands of acres of the ranches. The smaller lots were ideal for grain crops and enhanced the conversion of the valley's economy.

A map of Murray Township in eastern Alameda County, dated two years after the land boom, shows the owners of every plot, including sections that were either sold or unsold by McLaughlin.[60] The most desired land for both speculation and agriculture around Livermore went before the map's publication. McLaughlin retained many of the sections south and east of town, especially in the hillier country. The map shows the Bernals' plots and the Livermore school district which was larger than the plated town.

Mendenhall's plot No. 18, containing the town, is clearly indicated. Several other plots of the Bernal estate appear in the names of William Mendenhall's brothers, Martin and Absalom.

At the time the map was drawn, the descendants of Livermore still had considerable holdings including Robert, Jr., 448 acres; Carlota, 396 acres; and Miligras, 969 acres. These are lettered plots on the township map and do not conform to the government section boundaries. It is interesting that Las Positas plot A is missing from the map, possibly sold before the deadline or disallowed by the commission. The numbered Bernal plots are shown as surveyed during the bankruptcy. Some sections sold by McLaughlin that remained uncultivated or developed were later listed for sale at 25 to 50 percent above McLaughlin's prices. With successful crops and high income, the practicing farmers looked to increase their holdings, thus driving up the land prices. An editorial in the newspaper complained about getting many complaints from prospective buyers about the high prices.[61]

McLaughlin grew extremely rich from the land sales. He never reimbursed subcontractor Cox for his $50,000 out-of-pocket expenses building the first 20 miles of the WP. Cox sued McLaughlin who bought out the courts, including the Supreme Court, on seven occasions.[62] Cox eventually walked into McLaughlin's office and shot him dead.[63] Cox was not tried but instead declared a hero.[64] McLaughlin was by then almost universally hated. He also created the Pacific Gas Company which became today's Pacific Gas and Electricity (PG&E). Cox finally received his construction expenses from the McLaughlin estate after more than twenty-five years of legal wrangling.[65]

Initial settlement in Livermore was dominated by those moving over from Laddsville. The land boom created a significant increase in the surrounding farming population which created a rapid growth of the town's businesses. It also encouraged the settlement of immigrants.

The Livermore Hook and Ladder Volunteer Fire Company was formed in 1874 serving both Livermore and Laddsville. The company, supported by local businessmen, was formed by Bardellini and J. H. Mahoney. It initially had about thirty members. They bought a fire cart and constructed a firehouse with a 500-pound bell in the cupola.[66] The bell was rung to call the volunteer firefighters and also served to signal the start of a children's curfew. They started an annual ball with their own band.[67] The band also played at other events in town.

Andrew McLeod platted a subdivision on the Las Positas side of Lizzie Street between East First Street and what is now East Avenue. He had a deed for the property from before McLaughlin's claimed deadline. He filed a plat and was able to sell lots with proper deeds. Called the McLeod tract, it includes the present-day Saint Michael Church and Livermore High School. The subdivision's streets align with Lizzy Street on the Las Positas border rather than the streets in Mendenhall's plat. Church Street led to the Catholic chapel across the track in Laddsville. McLeod owned a general store, a saloon, and was postmaster. He became Livermore's first mayor then elected again two years later.

Early rancher Alexander Esdon owned Bernal Plot No. 17 just north of the WP track and platted an extension of the town known as the Northern Addition. It encompassed the area between I and P streets and from the railroad's right-of-way to Pine Street.[68] He built a kiln and started making bricks on his land. By the time the town was incorporated, Esdon's brickworks were making hundreds of thousands of dollars a year and employed twenty-five. He constructed several buildings which became known as the brick block. One of these buildings was to house a general store for Waterman and Company of San José on the corner of Railroad and Livermore avenues. It was, for years, the largest brick building in town. The store failed in 1889, and the building became the Farmers Union, with a 650-seat theater. It is rumored that the theater hosted the first American performance of Gilbert and Sullivan's Mikado.[69] It was demolished in 1929.[70] Two of his smaller buildings exist to this day in what is called Blacksmith Square.

Little news was published about the valley before the railroad. During the construction of the WP, all eyes were on Livermore Pass, Alameda Canõn, and occasionally the goings-on in Laddsville. News from outside came slowly, much delayed by wagon, horseback, or word of mouth. Newspapers from nearby cities were occasionally carried by the Butterfield Mail Stage. Butterfield was the president of Wells Fargo at the time the stage line was initiated. With the railroad newspapers suddenly became available on the day they were published, and mail delivery became faster and more reliable. The telegraph also provided much of the latest news.

With no local newspaper, only news that was of interest to their readers was published in the out-of-town papers. Local news was often relegated to an inside or back page. Marriages and deaths were announced when they involved someone with connections to the town where the paper was published.

Local interesting events occasionally appeared in the papers of neighboring towns. The following article was published in the *Sacramento Daily Union*. Second-class Pullman cars, later just called sleepers, had bench seating which converted to upper and lower bunk beds. Men and women shared the same cars, which occasionally led to interesting situations. For example, happenings in the darkness of the Livermore Pass tunnel:[71]

An incident took place on the overland train yesterday, while approaching Livermore's Pass on its way to this city, which was the source of great amusement to the passengers on one of the sleeping cars. A young man, who had worn his Chicago "cheviot" all the way through until that article of apparel was neither seemly or starchy, was expecting friends to meet him at Niles Station. He was anxious to make as good appearance before them as possible and decided on a change of linen. He had been over the road before and knew of the tunnel and just how long it required to go through it. He would make his change while the train was underground, and where no eye could pierce the darkness. With great deliberation he opened his traveling bag, took from it a "clean boiled rag" and placed it on the seat. The sleeve buttons were inserted, and the garment was placed in the required position. Then he calmly removed his necktie, unbuttoned his coat, ready in the instant for the coming tunnel. His movements had attracted no attention, and he was smiling with anticipation of the change with which he would startle his soot begrimed fellows. A whistle and the train plunges into a darkness impenetrable and almost oppressive. The train rattles on, then emerges into the light upon the other side. Behold the picture. With head and arms covered with the fluttering garment our hero struggles in the agony of despairing chagrin. He had forgotten to unbutton the collar, and of course he could not take off the shirt in the presence of the ladies. Amid a general yell of laughter, he subsided under the seat, where a friendly porter came and unbuttoned him.

The *San Jose Mercury-News* noted in 1873 that a newspaper called the *Independent Defender* was about to be started in Livermore.[72] No evidence remains of that effort. The first weekly newspaper of note began publishing in the valley for more than four years after the town was formed. The *Livermore Enterprise* was started by George Shearer and Charles Leys on May 16, 1874, and survived until the end of 1876. It was four pages published weekly on Saturdays. Half the paper was filed with local advertisements. Local news about individuals, property transactions, crimes, accidents, and fires, etc. were generally reported as one or a few sentences on the inside pages. Editorials and important local articles, occasional county, state or national news were generally on page two. Editorial comment was often mixed in with the facts in larger articles. The front page was half filled with advertisements. Front-page articles appear to be mostly fillers of undated general interest to farmers, editorials, and even poetry.

The *Enterprise* gave credence to the earlier comment in the *San Jose Mercury*, "of whisky mills innumerable." There were seven advertisements for the saloons and whisky mills in the first edition of the *Enterprise*. Few alcoholic beverages were imported and most establishments used local agricultural products to make their own beer, wine, and whisky. Articles about the many ownership and locations changes of the saloons appeared as one liners in a back page of the paper and were usually much smaller than the advertisements.

The bankrupt *Enterprise* was bought out by William P. Bartlett and renamed *The Livermore Herald*. Its format was initially similar to the *Enterprise* and was published weekly on Wednesdays beginning in 1877. It essentially continued the four-page format of the *Enterprise*. The *Herald's* building was later destroyed by fire and the newspaper was sold to Arthur

Henry.[73] Subsequently, Arthur's son, Maitland, carried on as the publisher and editor until 1956.[74] By the turn of the century, additional pages were added to the paper and leading news was moved to the front page. The *Livermore Echo* was started by Wilbur Still, as a monthly and then as a weekly on Thursdays from 1877 to 1919. Its format was four pages, similar to the *Enterprise*.

The Herald reported Livermore was still a rough-and-tumble place:

> Two tramps made their appearance in town, Sunday morning, and their perambulations about the streets being closely watched by some of our citizens, one of them was heard to exclaim to his comrade: "Well, Bob, let's git out of this durned place; them are watchmen be a looking us as though we wuz a travelin menagerie!" And they meandered off.

The newspapers chronicled the development of the town: shops opening and closing, buildings being erected and burning down, the formation of clubs, sports teams, births, weddings, and deaths. They also chronicled discriminatory acts towards the Natives, Chinese and Blacks. The advertisements in the early editions of both the *Enterprise* and *The Herald* show a significant change in the commercial development of the town in the two years leading to incorporation. There were more lawyers, doctors, druggists, general shops, and saloons once the town was incorporated. *The Herald* initially grouped advertisements for doctors, attorneys and then saloons in that order on page one in column one.[75]

The newspapers regularly reported on both domesticated and wild animals. Horses were necessary to pursue people's businesses and lives. Their achievements, capabilities, and serious injuries were most often reported. Dogs served people as companions, aids, and provided advanced warning of dangers. They were noted for their special capabilities and later trained as sled dogs for the Alaska gold rush.[76] Dogs were poisoned at times either intentionally or in the false belief they were unwanted critters.[77] Cattle and sheep were reported when large numbers trampled crops or suffered from drought and heat. There are multiple reports of mountain lions and lynx, as well as their kittens, being killed whenever they were seen.[78] Domestic cats were almost never reported as they were mostly left to do their own thing, eliminating rodents.

The telegraph brought in with the railroad opened rapid communication. It provided the ability to quickly order materials and supplies as well as breaking news from the rest of the country. The dispatch announcing the death of President Garfield was heard by J. L. Mitchel, as it flew over the wires about eight o'clock on a Monday evening. The news soon spread and within a few minutes, the bells of the Engine House and Presbyterian church began tolling out the age of the dead chief magistrate.[79]

Telegraph lines were strung around downtown. A line between the depot and post office allowed the weather predictions from the U.S. Signal Service to be posted daily.[80] Anspacher's, McLeod's, and Waterman's facilities later also connected into the telegraph line to expedite ordering.

Several property owners introduced the concept of incorporating the town. There were considerable loud arguments both for and against incorporation at a special meeting to vote on the proposal. A quote in the newspaper of those against it noted, "The bugbear of increased taxation and ruination is folly to the business portion of our community."

Property owners voted 26 for incorporation and 22 against.[81] The borders of the town were defined and the charter bill drafted and sent to Sacramento in just over a month.[82] Beazell, one of the founding commercial property owners and now a state senator, introduced the bill to the legislature. It was formally incorporated when the bill was signed by Governor William Irwin on April 1, 1876.[83]

4

FARM TOWN

Livermore's incorporation was briefly noted in two sentences on the second page of the *Enterprise* on April 15, 1876: "The act of incorporation of this place as a town has properly passed both Houses of the legislature, and has been signed by Governor Irwin. All that is now required is the election of the necessary local officers."[1]

The election several weeks later was held at the firehouse on Second Street. Two tickets on the ballot were called the "Regular" and "Tax Payers Town." They were composed of prominent citizens on opposing sides of the taxation arguments. Members of both tickets were nominated as trustees. The election results were announced in the *Enterprise* after the following introduction: "THE MAIDEN ELECTION, These country elections are funny things—queer excitements—pistols and coffee—disputes and whisky. Who invented elections?"[2]

Those elected included A. J. (Andrew) McLeod, J. Bowles, N. B. Holmes, M. Hupers, R. M. Caughell; also elected were R. B. Campbell, marshal, and H. Bailey, assessor. McLeod became the first chairman and mayor. The incorporation, including the Northern and McLeod subdivisions, created a town more than double its original size.

Laddsville was just a few private properties, and the Catholic Church are shown on the 1878 map, but were outside the town limits at the time of the incorporation. At the time, the town had 830 residents and 234 buildings within 840 acres.[3] The map shows no direct road crossing the rails to the Northern Addition. Access was via Laddsville. The only crossing was at East First Street as it entered Laddsville. However, the location for a crossing at Livermore Avenue is apparent.

The trustees met in the International Order of Odd Fellows' hall for the first year. They then moved into the firehouse on Second Street when it became city property.

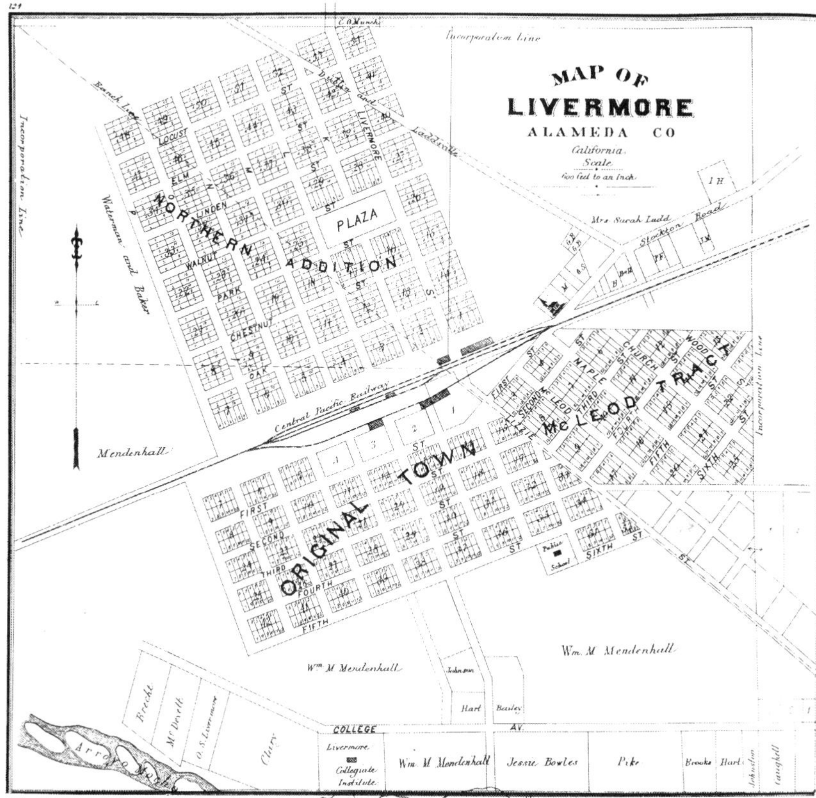

Three subdivisions of the 1876 incorporation published two years later, along with Laddsville and properties south of town. (*Thompson and West, 1878*)

Trustees of the town council established a comprehensive governing structure for the town within the first few months. Rules of order were adopted at the first meeting.[4] Property taxes to support the town were set at 50 cents per $100 assessed valuation. The tax was reviewed annually by the council but not changed for decades. The trustees adopted a town seal based on a plow and a sheaf of wheat.[5] The sheaf of wheat on the town seal was indicative of the agricultural revolution created by McLaughlin.

The town council passed ordinances creating paid positions for town clerk, attorney, treasurer, marshal, and fire chief. Several standing committees including finance, ordinance, streets and highways, and public morals.[6] The ordinances created regular meetings, salaries of officers, property taxes and required all businesses, laundries, saloons, shooting galleries, theatrical and musical performances, etc. to be licensed for a fee. Business licensing was established with fees prorated by their estimated monthly sales. Schools and churches were not required to be licensed. The owner turnover and relocation of saloons made their license applications one of the most numerous items in the trustees' agenda.

The trustees regularly met in the Hook and Ladder Company firehouse on Second and L streets. The town purchased the building from the fire company six years later, which then became known as the town hall. The meeting hall and justice court were on the second floor above the fire station below.[7]

Other ordinances were passed prohibiting unruly or obscene behavior, large animals running free in town, licensing excavation on public property, etc. An ordinance was also passed limiting the speed of trains passing through town to 8 mph but exempting passenger trains. The ordinances were all published in the local newspaper.

William Mendenhall and his wife, Mary, moved to Livermore from Santa Clara shortly after the town was incorporated and built a house on College Avenue in 1877. He was elected to the town council and later became mayor. He lived in town into his eighties. Shortly before his death in 1911, he moved in with his daughter in Oakland.[8] His wife, Mary, had died in 1903.[9]

Mendenhall donated plots along Fifth Street when the one-room School Street building became inadequate. A bond issue was passed to move the school to Fifth Street and construct a new building.[10] The building was finished the following year, and the original building was moved downtown to become a saloon.[11] The Fifth Street site hosted the Livermore Grammar School and three generations of public school buildings. Author Jack London lived in Livermore for three years as a child. He attended the Fifth Street Grammar School starting in 1883.[12] The most recent building on the site is the current Fifth Street School.

The first fire company in Livermore, Hook and Ladder Company No. 1, was formed and an engine purchased two years before incorporation. It was funded privately by thirty members of the town. The founders included Anton Bardellini whose hotel previously burned in Laddsville. They built a two-story firehouse with a bell tower on the south side of Second Street, between K and L streets.

Niagara Fire Engine No. 1 was later purchased by several members of the town. It initially became a second and separate fire company, started about six weeks after the town's incorporation. The town council passed an ordinance merging the two private companies becoming the Livermore Fire Department and appointing the chief and assistant.[13] The company members were volunteer, although in later years, the town provided $150 a month for some remuneration.[14]

Shortly afterwards, another fire in Laddsville destroyed Joseph Muna's Hotel, despite the efforts of the newly formed fire company. Laddsville businesses destroyed by fires were mostly rebuilt in Livermore. The trustees commissioned the water company to install three fire hydrants in Livermore and one in Laddsville.

At the same time, the fire company's brass band was rechartered as the Livermore Brass Band. It was largely comprised of members of the fire departments.[15]

Law enforcement was provided by the county marshal until the town was incorporated. One of the first tasks of the trustees was to instruct the town marshal to create a police department and take the necessary steps to use the county lock-up for town purposes. The marshal also acted as the tax collector. Initially, two volunteer policemen served as night watchmen. Within three years, the department grew to four policemen and had a calaboose built.[16] It was 12-feet square with three cells and an office for the constable.[17] A draft of an ordinance to prohibiting the carrying of concealed weapons was proposed to the council but not passed.[18]

An historic overview of Livermore was presented in a speech by *Enterprise* newspaper partner Charles Leys, celebrating the nation's centennial on the 4th of July. Leys' speech emphasized the significant growth of the town since its inception:

In this the Centennial year, the following may be taken as a synopsis of the Town of Livermore as It now is: Area Of the town 950 acres nearly with resident population of 830 souls, occupying 234 buildings, 148 of which are private houses, 91 being classed as follows: one post office, seven general stores, one dry goods, two tailors, four milliners. two laundries, three shoemakers, two bakeries one flour mill, four butchers, three fruiteries, two cabinet makers and undertakers, four blacksmiths, one tin and stove store, one architect and builder, one lumber yard, one water co. workshop, two harness makers, three Jewelers, one stationer, two photographers, four barbers, four livery stables, thirteen saloons, six hotels, one brewery, one soda factory, four doctors, two druggists, one dentist, three grain warehouses, one engine house, one printing office, three public halls, one Justice Court, four lawyers, one jail, one public school, one fine College Institute, two churches, one passenger and freight depot, one railroad office. We have two coal and two water companies.[19]

Saloons had proliferated in Laddsville and became the largest number of businesses in Livermore. Most made their own beer, whisky, and, occasionally, wine from local farm products. There were not many national liquor suppliers, and only the most expensive drinks could be imported. Several saloons also called themselves breweries. What they brewed was generally not very good and today would be characterized as "rot gut." Some also sold tobacco and seegars (spelling as advertised).[20]

Wendel Jordan, a recent German immigrant, bought Charles Schwerin's saloon and brewery in 1875. Jordan renamed his business the Livermore Brewery which became one of the most prominent in town. Jordan started producing a first-class lager beer and quickly started selling his beer to other saloons in bottles and kegs. The demand for Livermore Beer rapidly increased because of its good quality. He daily shipped large quantities of beer to various towns along the railroad. The beer later was regarded as the best in Alameda County. After Jordan's death, the brewery was sold to Dennis Bernal and continued in business until it was destroyed by fire in 1908. The *U. S. Health Bulletin*, a hygienic journal of New York, gave a very high recommendation of the beer made by Bernal.[21]

Soda pops and seltzer were not yet broadly available nationally. The Livermore Soda Works was formed and advertised as "Soda Water, Sassapharilla, Ginger Ale, Etc." (spelling as advertised). They were successful and later supplied other towns by rail. They concentrated on seltzer water to which flavors were added. Through multiple owners and a name change to the Livermore Beverage Company, they continued bottling seltzer until the company was destroyed by fire in 1966.[22]

Small stores selling certain foodstuffs were built downtown along First Street. Bakeries, butcher shops, and fruit and vegetable stands sold fresher and better-quality edibles than the general stores. A dairy was started, and fresh milk was for sale for the first time after the town's incorporation. The increasing number of farms sold a greater variety of fresh local foods. The availability of ice at 3 cents a pound made these shops possible. Small specialty stores proliferated, such as clothing, furniture, dry goods, jeweler and watchmaker, saddle and shoemakers, livery stables, blacksmiths, etc. Most of the small downtown stores carried multiple product lines. Schlesinger's Book and Stationery store also sold cutlery, toys, musical instruments, cigars, pipes, and tobacco.[23] The proliferation of shops was curbed by the limited number of buildings with substantial rent or property cost in the small-sized downtown. Those run by the early settlers, property owners and their families tended to survive, whereas those started by newcomers had high turnover.

Heavy and expensive farm equipment was being developed across the country but was not ordinarily carried by the general stores. They were brought to the attention of the farmers by traveling salesmen at the depot. They were ordered and procured as needed by Ansbacher's or through Station Agent Mitchel, communicating with the manufacturers by telegraph. Waterman's attempted to enter this business before it failed.

Some small items of farm equipment were invented and manufactured by the blacksmiths. The only early business in town still identifiable was the Victor and Harris Men's Clothing which became Victor and Baughman's. It is currently Baughman's Western Outfitters on First Street.

Laddsville and Livermore were on the road to the Central Valley and Sierra Gold Country, a fast one day's ride from the Bay Area. Two additional hotels were established in Laddsville after Ladd built his. The two hotels were destroyed by fire then rebuilt along First Street in Livermore. Ladd's hotel was later also destroyed by fire but not rebuilt. Several years later there were six hotels in Livermore.

Restaurants were almost nonexistent as many saloons also served food. The Oyster and Chop House was the back room of the Exchange Saloon advertising meals at all hours.[24] The hotels had their own dining facilities advertised as restaurants. The Washington Hotel advertised an Italian restaurant.

Fredrick Mally opened a shoe repair business in Laddsville before Livermore was formed. His business was burned out in the 1871 fire, and he started a new business in Livermore. He built a store on the south side of First Street between J and K streets where he expanded to selling fancy goods.[25] His family lived in the building, and there were a couple of extra rooms that were rented to roomers. By the turn of the century, the store had become a grill, saloon and inn. His son, Clarence, took over the business after his father's death. The grill became well known in the first half of the twentieth century for its special events as well as good food and low prices.[26]

In the sparsely populated Laddsville and early Livermore, the first doctors also ran a drugstore. Their primary income was through trade for services and the sale of other items such as guns and ammunition. Fifteen years after incorporation, the *Echo* reported: "Livermore now has four practicing physicians and three dentists, to attend to the health and the condition of the masticating machinery of its people."[27] Three years later, the number of physicians had grown to six.

Some doctors used their drugstores as their offices, while others developed independent and more extensive facilities. Their main medical tasks were the treatment of wounds and burns caused by accidents and fires. The procedures for such treatments and surgeries evolved greatly during the Civil War. Livermore's doctors usually treated injuries and minor surgeries in their offices. Cases requiring major surgery had to be sent to other communities as there was no hospital in Livermore for decades.

There were some medications to alleviate symptoms, but little to actually cure a disease. Doctors' prescriptions usually were a chemical formula to be prepared by a druggist. The concept of microbes being germs for disease was beginning to be understood, though no medications had yet been developed.

Some so-called druggists were actually snake oil salesmen. S. Hereinghi opened a shop on First Street claiming to have a complete assortment of drugs, chemicals, and patent medicines. He was the Livermore agent for Dr. Steele's Medical Wonder, advertised to purify the blood and cure rheumatism, neuralgia, headache, cramp, lame back, chills, fever, and external and internal aches and pains.[28] Years later, C. D. Hall rented the store next to the Livermore Hotel for the sale of Radam's Microbe Killer, a specific for rheumatism, cancers, and an endless variety of heretofore considered to be incurable diseases.[29]

Drugstores sold more than just chemicals and medications. Some also sold perfumery and a variety of toilet articles. N. Grey manufactured and sold writing inks at his drugstore. Similarly, dentists doubled as barbers for a more reliable income than occasionally pulling teeth. No treatment had yet been developed for smallpox, tuberculosis, diphtheria, scarlet fever, typhoid, measles, mumps and whooping cough, etc. Isolation was recognized to limit their spread. The concept of healing waters and fresh air were widely considered to aid the treatment of many diseases, most prominently tuberculosis. Six cottages were erected at the Agua de Vida Springs, for the accommodation of those who desired the virtues of the fresh air and healing waters.[30] They hosted forty-two guests a month later and began to make the Livermore area known for its relief of symptoms.

The council hired a health officer and defined the duties to recommend rules and regulations regarding health and sanitation.[31] The officer was authorized to require quarantines and school closures to limit the spread of diseases.

The Livermore Library and Dramatic Association initiated a subscription and donation funded library shortly after the town was incorporated. It was first housed in a jewelry store and then moved to a larger furniture store as it grew. The Livermore Public Library Association was formed and converted the earlier library to a free public facility.[32]

Calvin J. Stevens donated a property on First Street, and a small structure was built to house the library in 1878.[33] It is likely that early newspapers were donated to the library which was responsible for preserving them.

The streets in town were hot and dusty in summer and were muddy and often flooded after heavy winter rains in winter. Homeowners began spreading gravel on the streets by their lots to reduce the dust and mud issues.[34] It became apparent that the streets needed grading. The county's roads funds were limited and could only cover minimum maintenance hence.

The trustees created a standing committee for streets and roads at their third meeting after incorporation.[35] The significant dust along L Street caused the council to order 4 inches of gravel for 8 feet on either side of the center line between Second and Fifth streets.[36] $25 was subsequently appropriate to pay for the gravel contract. Several months later, the council contracted for the installation of eight oil-burning streetlamps. The night watchman was charged with lighting and maintaining the lamps.

The streets were officially declared public highways which transferred maintenance and upgrading from the individual property owners to the town.[37] Street improvement such as grading, graveling, adding wooden sidewalks and drainage were expensive tasks. The improvement of First Street from Lizzie to L streets, with a cost of $100, was approved by the council.[38] This cost was significant when the town's total income for the year was $4,022, and the year-end balance was $219.02.[39] Installing 800 feet of concrete sidewalks along First Street was later considered a major achievement.

Adjacent property owners were assessed for the improvements of their streets. Major street flooding occurred regularly with heavy winter rains. This required the construction of culverts and the digging of ditches to direct the water to the arroyos. The railroad was accommodating in providing culverts under the tracks.

The improvements and spreading gravel continued street by street for many years and were still far from complete by the turn of the century. Sprinkling water on streets, especially those not graveled, was widely used to help keep down the dust.

There were no road bridges crossing the creeks. Pulling a wagon or riding a horse across a creek was dangerous or even deadly when flooded. The arroyos Mocho and Valle were both unfordable at times of high water. The footbridges crossing the Mocho at L Street were twice carried away by water in less than two months. This caused a deal of inconvenience and complaints. "When will the powers that be give us needed bridges instead of everlastingly hauling gravel?"[40]

The college organized a baseball team which played other teams from the Bay Area. Baseball was all the rage across the nation, and Livermore was not far behind. The fire department, newspapers, and some of the business leaders all supported teams.

Ansbacher's opened a baseball field on an empty First Street lot west of the store. Other fields were also opened around town. The newspapers along with the school started a junior league. Games were played against teams from other schools around the area. By the turn of the century, the best local teams were playing throughout the Bay Area. Livermore fields were better in the winter so regional professional teams came in for spring practice. The Livermore Baseball Club grounds was referred to in the *Enterprise* as "no doubt one of the best baseball grounds in the state." Other sports did not grow up in town until after the turn of the century.

Quite a few associations, clubs, lodges, and societies supporting sporting, social, artistic, religious, and commercial interests were formed through the years. Some of these included a post of the Grand Army of the Republic veterans association, the Benevolent Society, a Grove of Druids, a German-speaking club, a farmers' club, The League of Progress, the Foresters, Masons, Liberal Union, the Women's Christian Temperance Union, the Lyceum League and Dramatic Club, Young Men's and Ladies' Institutes, Woodmen of the World, Pioneers of the Valley, Native Sons and Daughters, Merchants Retail and Commercial Agency, Sons of Hermann, and more. There were so many organizations that members of the town often belonged to several.

Balls were among the most popular forms of evening entertainment before the turn of the century. The first and largest was the Fireman's Ball annually produced as a fundraiser. Fundraising balls became quite common among many non-profit associations and clubs. Some balls organized by individuals were purely social events. Performances by college students and groups, as well as visiting artists, provided considerable evening entertainment.

A temperance league was formed and sponsored a local plebiscite to limit liquor sales. After incorporation the number of saloons had more than doubled since the earliest years. An editorial in the *Enterprise* noted that saloons represented a significant portion of the town's economy. The *Herald* editor commented, "the town should not be lead by a lot of vain and notoriety seeking silly women."

The all-male electorate defeated the proposition.[41] Towns throughout the county were encouraged to make their own "wet-dry" decision almost forty years later. At that time, an Anti-Saloon League was formed and lobbied for a dry town. Livermore again voted to turn down limits on alcohol sales.[42]

A petition was presented to the council signed by forty-eight ladies of the town. They prayed for the closing of saloons after 10 p.m. each day.[43] A proposed ordinance preventing the sale of liquor and opening saloons after 10 p.m. each day was defeated by the council at the following meeting. Two years later, an ordinance was again considered that all businesses, including saloons, be closed between 12 a.m. and 4 a.m.

Several meetings were conducted advocating women's suffrage, but attendance was only fair.[44] The Ladies League of Progress formed to support the library and refused to support a female suffrage amendment to state constitution.[45] More than twelve years later, a state constitutional amendment, giving women the right to vote, narrowly passed election with only 50.7 percent of the vote.[46]

After the town was incorporated, the *Livermore Enterprise* newspaper noted important shipments, including 160 tons of coal shipped in a week,

700 tons of wheat and barley, upwards of 220 head of beef cattle, 5,760 dozen eggs, 1,000 pounds of butter, five carloads of wool, and three carloads of flour. J. L. Mitchel reported the shipment of treasure for the month of March 1875, gold notes, $2,030; currency, $1,015.94; gold, $3,057; silver, $4,040; total: $10,132.94.[47]

At harvest times, crops were being harvested faster than they could be shipped by ten or more rail carloads a day. The increased number of warehouses were able to largely even the flow and were of small cost to the farmers. Station Agent Mitchel reported that nearly two million pounds of hay, wheat, barley, oats, and flour were shipped from Livermore in 1880.[48] The value of hay was only a couple of cents per pound, the grains had greater value bringing in considerable income for the farmers. The markups and the large amounts reported to have been shipped created considerable profits for the warehouses' owners.

Many Chinese workers who had arrived during the gold rush were not welcomed into the Civil War armies, local society, or employment even when white labor was scarce. They were reluctantly used in the construction of the railroad. Some Chinese railroad workers later settled in Livermore. Some worked as laborers on nearby farms. The blocks bordered by First, Second, P, and Q streets, settled by former railroad construction workers, became known as Chinatown.[49]

An early editorial in the *Enterprise* did much to inflame anti-Chinese attitudes, "We don't approve of these moon-eyed sons of the west taking the jobs of white men."[50]

A petition was circulated to have a lease revoked for a Chinese washhouse.[51] Anti-Chinese meetings were held at the Union Hall.[52] The town trustees passed an ordinance outlawing opium possession or smoking, apparently aimed at the Chinese.[53] The Chinese were shunned from farm work. A gang of about fifty Chinese men were engaged in clearing out the ditches along the line of the railroad.[54] Road construction and laundries became about the only businesses they were allowed and most eventually left the town. Stanford supported restrictive legislation against indigenous people, Chinese, and Blacks.[55]

One of history's most consequential and moral questions came before the California Legislature. The state assembly and senate were asked to ratify the 15th Amendment to the United States Constitution, which would guarantee nonwhite Americans the right to vote. The text was short and to the point, stating that the right of U.S. citizens to vote could not be denied or abridged on the basis of "race, color or previous condition of servitude." For the amendment to be adopted, three-quarters of the thirty-seven American states needed to vote yes. Both houses of the California Legislature voted no in January 1870. The legislature did not vote to accept the amendment until 1962.[56] The federal government passed the Chinese Exclusion Act in 1882. Chinese were prevented from voting and becoming citizens. Additional immigrants from China were prevented from entering the United States for ten years. The law was later revised to be permanent until it was repealed in 1943.

Agriculture, eventually including winemaking, played an important role in Livermore's history. Robert Livermore is said to have been the first to grow grapes and make wine for his own use in the valley as early as 1849. An experienced winemaker, J. M. Tellis suggested that the Livermore Valley was ideal for growing grapes and making wine. In his 1881 letter to the *Herald*, he pointed out that wine making would be more profitable than ranching and grain farming. He subsequently leased the Ladd vineyard and moved to the valley.[57] A review article in the *Herald* noted: "In February 1881, there was not in the Livermore Valley a vineyard of any size, though there might be a few scattered acres of grapes, put in by men who wished to make a few hundred gallons of wine for their own use."[58] The following year, Julius P. Smith bought and planted a vineyard he called Olivina.

The first shipment of native fruit from Livermore station consisted of seventeen boxes of grapes, from the Robinson vineyard. Charles Wetmore, the chief viticultural officer of the State Viticultural Commission, explored the valley and started the Ojo del Monte vineyard; he also planted olives. He moved to the valley and became the senior proponent for local winemaking.[59] His holdings were later consolidated into what became known as Cresta Blanca Vineyards. Various other small vineyards were established at that time. James Concannon founded his winery in 1883. Carl Wente bought a half interest in a small winery in 1884 and later acquired full ownership.

Concannon had significant business in Mexico before establishing the winery. Later, needing capital for the winery, he arranged the support of President Porfirio Diaz to improve the Mexican wine business. He shipped rail car loads of grapevine cuttings to Mexico.[60] The shipments were of sufficient interest to be regularly reported in the local newspapers.[61]

Mumm, the purveyor of French champagne and wine, claimed that California wines could not be as good as the French. Charles Wetmore was asked to join a committee to respond in the New York newspapers.[62] His Cresta Blanca Winery's Sauvignon Blanc won the grand prize at the Paris Exposition in 1889. The railroad constructed a chute behind the freight depot for convenience in handling wine in puncheons, large barrels holding from 72 to 120 gallons, and other heavy freight.[63]

By 1893, there were 121 vineyards growing grapes in the valley on about 5,000 acres, with the grapes having an annual average value of $60 per acre.[64] By then, Livermore had shipped nearly 300,000 gallons of wine in one season.[65] The value of wine exported exceeded that of hay and grains grown in the valley. This represented a significant change in the agricultural basis of the valley's economy.

Sheep and cattle drivers were careless when crossing the newly planted vineyards and caused considerable damage. Small numbers of livestock were transported to markets by train. Most large herds of sheep and cattle were still driven to distant ranches or pastures. In one incident, 10–15 acres of the Olivina vineyard were devastated.[66] "Livermore was invaded last Sunday evening, by a band of 1,000 head of cattle, on their way from Hollister to Stockton. Two thousand more are on their way."

The weekly newspaper, the *Livermore Echo*, in its section called *Local Echoes*, recorded much of the comings and goings at the station. Arbitrarily opening the newspaper to Thursday, August 11, 1897, on page three, we find the following:

A. Duval received two carloads of cooperage on Monday. A. G. Cauche shipped two carloads of wine on Tuesday. Eighty passenger tickets were sold at the Depot last Monday. Livermore Gas Company received ten carloads of coal yesterday. Herta and Kennedy yesterday received ten carloads of lumber. S. Bordia received two full-blooded Newfoundland pups by express yesterday morning.

Train schedules were constantly advertised in the local newspapers. Equipment and crews of regular trains were rarely altered. Conductors and engineers took personal responsibility for their train and service to the community. Local train crews that regularly served the town became well known by name in the community. Their lives and adventures were followed in the local newspapers:

Engineer Bradley of the Livermore Local had a narrow escape from being wrecked, in Niles Canyon. Rain had been falling during the afternoon, and sometime after dark, a slide occurred covering the track with rock and earth. Coming around the curve Bradley instantly reversed the engine, applied the air brakes, and then, seeing a strike was inevitable, jumped free of the machine. The engine struck the slide like a battering ram, scattering rocks pall mall, right and left. He had jumped down a high, steep bank, and, strange to say, escaped with but a few severe bruises. He was found about a quarter of a mile behind, trudging after the train. The train had stopped safely and was delayed but 20 minutes. Engineer Bradley has recovered from the effects of his recent jump in the dark in Niles Canyon, and again pulls the throttle on the engine of our morning and evening local.[67]

The newly adopted air brakes prevented a more serious incident.

Local telephone companies were beginning to be established in 1884, and interconnects were being considered to neighboring towns. Ranchers in the hills east of town formed the Altamont Barbed Wire Telephone Company. They used their fence wire lines to interconnect their telephone service. The initial line connected the Young Ranch on North Flynn Road with the Sweet Ranch on Patterson Pass Road. The line became the first rural phone line in Northern California and operated for more than thirty years.[68] The railroad started its own internal service which paralleled its network of telegraph lines.

Later, a public phone with long-distance capability was provided at the depot. Electric lighting was becoming popular in the late 1880s. An early proposal by the Waterhouse Electric Company for a light plant in Livermore consisted of a dynamo and eleven mast-lights using arc lamps.[69] Jacob Hanna was granted an electric street lighting franchise by the city council a year later. Uses of electric power advanced through the decade. The Southern Pacific Company considered putting in electric bells that would give ample warning of approaching trains at the various crossings. Despite the promising note, it was still many years before warning signals were installed at crossings.

Mining was active in the hills south and east of town with ores brought to Livermore for shipment or local use. Mines Road made it possible to haul out ores without prohibitive expense.[70] Mined products included sand, gravel, clay bricks, coal, later lime rock, magnesite (magnesium carbonate), cinnabar (mercury), gypsum, manganese, and talc.[71] Coal was likely the most dangerous of all the mining operations with cave-ins, gas explosions, and fires. Silver discovered by Mendenhall near Livermore assayed at $80 per ton. Less profitable deposits of gold and chromium were reported.[72] Oil seeps were discovered and limited extraction continues to this day.[73]

Natural gas was often mixed with water in domestic wells. A letter from Livermore to *the Alameda Advocate* says that there is quite an oil excitement:

A well was sunk 55 feet when a gas commenced to issue which took fire (from a candle) and burned brilliantly. There is a constant roaring going on in the bottom of the well and the water in the well is as blue as indigo, and smells of coal oil and sulphur. The gravel that comes from the bottom of the well is covered with some bright metallic substance, the color of gold There is one thing sure, if there is nothing else, they have struck a bully gas mine.[74]

Gas was of sufficient amounts to be used for lighting, heating, and cooking throughout town. A company was organized to lay down and maintain gas lines in the streets. They mostly sold the gas for lighting. The town started installing gas streetlamps a few at a time as they could be afforded.[75]

Initially, burial grounds were on family properties. Oak Knoll Cemetery was started as the Mendenhall's family burial ground on a hill alongside Arroyo Mocho on Martin Mendenhall's property west of town. It was recognized as a public cemetery two years after the town's incorporation.

Publisher of the *Herald* and local real estate agent William Bartlett commissioned a perspective rendering of the town.[76] He had it printed as a poster and distributed it to advertise his real estate business. It is an aerial view and appears to be fairly accurate in locating and depicting existing structures, streets, and the railroad station as they existed in 1889. It is interesting to note that both the McLeod and Northern Additions were still sparsely settled because of limited population growth.

Livermore's original freight depot burned to the ground on June 28, 1891. The event occurred during the hottest weather recorded to date. The depot fire was thought to have begun with a case of gasoline exploding, caused by the excessive heat.[77] Due to increased usage, a more substantial depot was needed. The replacement depot, CP design No. 18, was the last of Arthur Brown's standard designs and completed in 1892. The new depot was a combined freight and passenger depot. It had a second story that provided living quarters for the station agent and his family. The standard design was 24-feet wide by 92-feet long. However, for Livermore, the freight house was twice the length of the standard, with an extended covered freight shed.

These variations reflected the vibrant and growing economy of Livermore. Few images of the depot from before the 1906 San Francisco earthquake exist today. A print on the wall of Mel Lemos' barbershop is thought to have been a copy by Elliot Dopking.[78]

The station track plan was significantly altered with the construction of the new depot. The old depots were located too close to the mainline for a house track in between. A house track is a siding that runs close to a loading dock so that cars can be loaded or unloaded without blocking the main track. Before the construction, the house track passed to the south of both the freight and passenger depots. The new depot was located further south of the main track, so there was room for a house track between the mainline and the depot. The part of the old house track west of L Street survived and became a siding connecting the spur into the turntable and engine house. The turntable was enlarged to accommodate the new larger locomotives. The siding later also served customers between the downtown siding and the mainline.[79]

The Livermore Collegiate Institute prospered with an average of fifty students annually for twenty years. George Pardee graduated from the

Livermore's Central Pacific Railroad Depot, built in 1892. (*Mel Lemos*)

school and later became California's governor. Mendenhall's daughter attended the school, and many of the graduates became teachers. The college closed when Livermore's free public high school was established.[80] The buildings and grounds were sold to Dr. Robertson, before the turn of the century and became part of the Livermore Sanitarium in 1896.[81]

The Livermore Union High School District was formed in 1891, becoming the first union high school district in the state.[82] The first high school was completed in 1893. The school district was later redefined as the Livermore Unified School District when the rural elementary and high school district boundaries were consolidated in 1966.[83]

During the Pullman strike, local rail service carrying the mail and newspapers continued to Livermore but became sporadic. The *Sacramento Daily Union*, the mouthpiece of the SP, accused the *Livermore Herald* of misinformation for an article calling for a peaceful resolution after troops were sent to Sacramento to quell the strike in 1894.[84]

Pleasanton, located 7 miles west of Livermore, is its nearest neighbor. It was the homestead of the Bernal cattle *ranchero* in the Valle de San José. It started as a village about the same time as Livermore, but it was not incorporated until 1894. The railroad ran through town, but it did not have the extensive station as Livermore. Sunol was also an early *ranchero* of the Mission San José at the head of Alameda Cañon (Niles

Livermore's first high school, completed in 1893. (*Livermore Heritage Guild*)

Canyon). It also became a village when the railroad came through, but it was never incorporated. It remains a village today. Other nearby towns, Dublin and San Ramon were not on the mainline nor incorporated until after the San Ramon branch of the railroad was completed in 1910.

The late nineteenth-century natives were described as unattractive, having dark complexion and small stature.[85] The change in description, as noted by Crespi, may have been due to the harsh conditions of the mission.

The last Indian settlement in the valley was established by Chief Tausino Sanchumi and his family near Pleasanton. He was well known and said to have been more than 100 years old. When he was young, he entered Mission San José and witnessed the development of the valley.[86] The family settlement survived after his death into the twentieth century. The settlement was visited by Edward Gifford in 1914 who reported their speaking the Miwok language.[87]

The Alaska gold rush created considerable interest in Livermore with several traveling there and staying a year or more. Returning from Alaska, D. B. Morrill reported that a number of Livermore folks were in Dawson. They were doing fairly well, though nearly all were working for wages.[88]

Livermore was not significantly affected by the 1890s depression. Growth of the town, although minimal, was largely driven by the growth

Chief Tausino Sanchumi, *circa* 1899. (*San Francisco Examiner*)

of commercial establishments, proliferation of smaller farming units, and the services necessary to support them. Limited new housing only slightly infilled the McLeod and Northern Additions.[89] Although there were fewer than 2,000 residents within the town lines of Livermore, it had a full spectrum of shops, financial, medical, and cultural services for the entire valley at the turn of the century.

5

MOGULS DOMINATE

Railroad ownership and function were dominated by the Wall Street moguls into the early twentieth century. Their interest was to maximize their personal profits by stock manipulation, increase holdings, and minimize competition. Their failures created national financial panics, bank closures, and depressions as they used large amounts of borrowed funds. They knew little about operations and left that to hired managers.

With the completion of the Pacific Railroad, the Associates did not have a viable business plan to bring in the funds necessary for both operations and service of its debts. Carrying passengers and the mail was required by law but was not profitable. Freight and the China trade were meant to be the profitable mainstays but were insufficient. Development and sale of adjacent grant properties to create both income and freight were viewed as the path to profitability. The development of so-called "railroad towns," such as Livermore, encouraged land sales and was seen as a future source of freight business.

WP depots at stations were designed by Arthur Brown (1830–1917). He was superintendent of bridges and buildings for the Associates until 1890. Brown developed a series of standard depot designs which evolved over the years. His designs were the basis of both the original and final Livermore depots. Initially, all the depots along the WP line were small and of a similar design. They were mostly all replaced by larger structures. The standard designs were adjusted in size to serve the expected needs of individual stations. The depots were delivered to the stations as kits that included all the necessary lumber, doors, windows, etc.

The early depots and other station buildings were all painted the same brown color. Brown specified the mixing instruction as a bucket of boiled linseed oil and a bucket of ground rust. The paint was fire resistant and later called "metallic." In the vernacular, however, it was referred to as "Arthur Brown." The depots had white trim and red roofs.

Standard design depots all mostly had the same facilities, including a passenger waiting room, an office for ticket sales and the station master, baggage, and freight rooms. Depots built later had a second story for a station master's apartment.

Differences in both passenger fares and freight rates for local and through services were significant. The railroad claimed its average rates for a ton to be carried a mile were on a par with Eastern railroads. However, there were higher rates where competition from boats did not exist as well as for trains in hilly country rather than flat. This was particularly irksome for Livermore farmers because the extra rates applied for both Niles Canyon, the Altamont as well as the lack of a navigable waterway in the valley.[1] It cost more to ship a ton of wheat to Oakland from Livermore than from Sacramento.[2] Even so the railroad rates were lower than commercial wagon drayage, thereby encouraged freight business.[3]

Passenger fares for local town to town service along the line were established on a per mile basis, whereas long-distance passenger fares were on a city-to-city basis and were significantly lower on a per mile basis. Trains cost about the same to run on a per mile basis no matter how many passengers were aboard.

Overland trains were a bit more expensive to run because they carried Pullman Palace cars. The general public, especially in a farming community, never traveled at all, even rarely to the next town. The second-class coach fares, although almost half the cost of first class, were still quite high for people who never had much in their pockets. Excursion specials with negligible ticket prices were a way to introduce large numbers of people to train travel. The $3 special fare to the State Fair was highly successful and packed the trains in the opening days of railroad service.

For only the first week, passengers from Oakland connecting with service to the East had a train change and lengthy wait in Sacramento. Thereafter, overland service was continuous from the San Francisco ferry. Connecting service between Oakland and San Jose required a time-consuming change of trains at the temporary San Jose Junction.[4] That junction, without amenities, was within Niles Canyon between the first and second bridges.

San Jose Junction was replaced the following year by Niles Junction. It was just west of Vallejo's Mill on railroad-purchased property. A new town, around the junction, was named for Judge Addison Niles, a friend of the Associates. The railroad subsequently identified Alameda Cañon as Niles Canyon. They also renamed Livermore Pass as the Altamont.

The Associates turned their attention to their own interests after completion of the railroad. They had little interest in and were inept at running a railroad. They were products and practitioners of the Gilded Age and were totally corrupt by today's standards. The Associates cultivated power and fortune by providing favors for their friends and expecting favors and loyalty in return. The favors included valuable stock options, loans, free transit passes on railroads, seats on boards of directors, and favorable court rulings. The complexity of the arrangements with their various friends and stockholders caused some deals not to be completed for years.

Huntington personally disliked Stanford. They operated differently and had different values. Collis Huntington, using bribes and intimidation, had become a stock manipulator and fixture in the railroad stock gaming era on Wall Street. He mostly relied upon spies and stock manipulation. Stanford built his political empire by using favors to friends, the courts, politicians, and toughs that he controlled. They also lived differently, Stanford with opulent mansions, farms, and racehorses and Huntington, the workaholic, in his tiny New York office.

McLaughlin concentrated his efforts on marketing and managing his land grants. Historian Richard White claims the Associates were really a political machine.[5]

A great concern for both the CP and UP was the Crédit Mobilier scandal. Thomas Durant, the flamboyant head of the UP, was just as corrupt as Huntington. Crédit Mobilier was the construction and money laundering arm of the UP principals, similar to the CP's Contract & Finance Company. A suit of UP stockholders opened the unsavory details of stocks being handed out or sold at advantageous prices to politicians. A congressional investigation was launched, and U.S. Marshals seized the UP's books. The vice president, speaker of the house, and several senators and congressmen were implicated in the scheme.

Representative Oaks Ames was censured for helping distribute the stock. The rest were conveniently forgotten in the election year.

Huntington's hermit-like existence and secretive dealings kept him out of the limelight for a while. He realized the Associates' jeopardy in the scandal, especially after obfuscating as a witness before Congress. He had the Associates quickly disband the Contract & Finance Company and burn its books before the Federal Marshals could get their hands on them.[6] The Western Development Company was formed and owned by the Associates to carry on the business.[7]

There was a boom in railroad building after the Civil War. Most of the construction used borrowed funds. The economy then fell into a depression in the 1870s as the Crédit Mobilier scandal was brewing. A major bank behind the railroad boom, Jay Cooke & Company, was no longer able to raise funds, and the subsequent bank failure caused a panic on the stock market. The depression took down many railroads, including the UP. The collapse and reorganization of the UP opened the door for Jay Gould, already infamous for cornering the gold market four years earlier, to lead the UP Board.[8] Through the next forty years, Gould and his son, George, would become major players in the national railroad scene.

Huntington could not borrow the funds necessary to pay the interest on the bonds. He did his best building railroads rather than running them, so his emphasis and interest was building the SP, not running or maintaining the CP. He placed the CP up for sale, but no offers emerged. Luckily, it was a profitable year for operations, especially as there was a bumper wheat harvest. Shipping revenues were sufficient to stave off bankruptcy.[9]

The second-level managers, with the occasional directive from the front office, established operational procedures and property policies. Train crews were assigned to specific runs no matter how far it went or how long it took. There were few work rules and little compensation. Safety was initially a concern for those building the railroad.

In the frontier, *rancheros* medical issues were mostly from sickness, fires, falls, gun shots, and various accidents involving horses, with or without wagons. New kinds of accidents came with the railroad. These caused injury or death to passengers, crew members and the general public. A hospital was built in Sacramento for sickness or injury of its employees before the railroad was completed. As a sort of insurance policy, employees and the officers were charged 50 cents a month to support the hospital. The Chinese workers were not covered by the policy.[10]

Injuries, including deadly accidents caused by primitive equipment were so common that they were initially considered just an occupational hazard or the risk of the journey. The accidents had little financial consequence for the railroads, consequently the hazardous conditions were rarely addressed by the owners or noted in the newspapers. Deadly accidents were more commonly reported. Although fires, collisions, and derailments were not as common, they created considerable delays, damage, and were costly to repair. They garnered greater attention from both the public and management.[11]

Accidents caused by poor communication and human error were also initially common. The most tragic accident on the WP occurred just days after the Oakland wharf and the route to it were opened in late 1869.[12] The Overland, at full speed on a track shared with the Oakland & Alameda Railroad, struck a local train head on, with devastating consequences. Seventeen people were killed and many more injured. Among the dead was U.S. District Judge Alexander Baldwin of Nevada. The cause was later determined to be an untrained switchman who prematurely let the Overland through before the local had cleared the track. The newly hired switchman, Bernard Kane, was initially arrested then released.[13]

This accident and others in these early months of operation were attributed to untrained workers and poor management in the rush to open service. Experience of dedicated long-term crew members and explicit operating rules reduced, but never fully eliminated, such accidents.

Poorly designed and operated locomotives started many fires which were sometimes costly. A fire damaged a bridge between Pleasanton and Livermore and delayed trains for several hours.[14]

The locomotives did not have their own brakes. They were stopped by the engineer reversing the driving wheels. Each car in a train had a handbrake operated by a wheel accessible on its roof. Whistle signals from the locomotive ordered the train crew to climb the cars to slow or stop the train. The conductors and brakemen had to walk on top of the train in motion, then jump from car to car to apply the brakes. Actions of the engineer or the uneven application of the brakes caused cars to slam together or apart due to slack in the sloppy couplings. The sudden impacts could be quite violent, causing crew or passengers to be injured and even thrown from the train with deadly consequences.[15]

The link-and-pin system to couple cars together required the hand placing of a chain link and dropping in a securing pin as the cars were being shoved together. Brakemen rarely survived with fingers intact. The *Stockton Independent* reported that on a freight train, not far from the Livermore tunnel, a coupling pin gave way, and the cars became separated, dividing the train. Capt. N. A. Green, the conductor, was thrown from the train and killed.[16] Slowing or stopping the train required the engineer to give sufficient advance warning and was almost useless in an emergency. When a passenger fell from a train at full speed near Livermore, it took a mile to stop the train.[17]

Eli Hamilton Janney invented the knuckle coupler, which engaged automatically when cars were shoved together.[18] The coupler made it unnecessary for a brakeman to go between the cars to couple or uncouple them. The couplers reduced the slack between the cars and later improvements eliminated it altogether.

George Westinghouse invented the air brake, whereby the engineer could set all the brakes on the train simultaneously with a single lever.[19] Hoses between and locomotive the cars provided a constant air pressure to the entire train. A reduction in the pressure set the brakes. If cars separated and the hose disengaged, all pressure would be lost and caused brakes on the entire train to set. The coupler and brake technologies both significantly reduced the injuries and deaths of trainmen and passengers alike. The new technologies also allowed heavier, longer, and faster trains.

The Southern Pacific Railroad (SP) existed in name only when it was taken over by the Associates. It was chartered by Congress after the Civil War as a land grant road to connect with and become part of a transcontinental network taking a southern route. Officially the CP and SP were separate railroads organized as separate corporations. The Associates' profits from the CP were illegally transferred to the SP through the Contract and Finance Company. Funding was mostly done through the Associates' own Western Development Company. It was, in effect, an illegal money laundry, transferring corporate assets from one company to another. The SP was to become the heart of Huntington's empire. However, because of stock holdings by others, it was kept as a separate company than the CP.

Huntington worked from New York, manipulating stock to defuse the threat of competition and surviving the economic morass he had created. His major effort concentrated on building the Southern Pacific and collecting the land grants. Feeder lines were not a threat but an opportunity for Huntington. They brought traffic and connections to his trunk lines. They were simpler to finance since profits or stock supported by a rich resource or a farming cooperative. They could more easily provide collateral for construction loans. Huntington allowed feeder lines to be built by their investors. If the lines were successful, he would find a way to take them over, subordinate their investors, then raise their freight and passenger rates. Huntington also illegally used CP profits for the acquisition of other roads. The SP was reorganized multiple times to incorporate more than fifty acquired lines. Huntington became president of the SP and eventually controlled the CP board as well. The Associates also organized a new company, the San Francisco Bay Railroad, to link the WP line to Oakland.

Locally, the California Pacific (Cal-P) was chartered by competitive San Francisco financiers. They started building from Sacramento to Vallejo along the northern side of the Carquinez Strait. Their goal was to bypass the WP line with a ferry to San Francisco, which would be both faster and cheaper to operate.[20] Huntington acquired the Cal-P with an under-the-table $250,000 bribe to take control of the Cal-P.[21]

The Associates also acquired the Northern Railway Company, which ran north along the Berkeley and Richmond waterfront. The CP extended track from Oakland, northeast along the Carquinez Strait to Port Costa and added a spur to the Cal-P across the Suisun Marsh to Benicia.[22] The Benicia to Port Costa Ferry rail service was started in 1879. The construction of two ferry slips and the world's largest rail ferryboat, the *Solano*, were another triumph for Arthur Brown, Sr. The *Solano* could carry a full twenty-four-car passenger train with locomotive.[23]

The new ferry service took 75 miles off the Sacramento to Oakland route and made it all at water level, bypassing the heavy grade over the

Altamont and the challenging Niles Canyon. Since the average train speed was 25 mph and the ferry crossing only took half an hour, it reduced the travel time by more than two hours. Suddenly, the former Western Pacific line through Livermore was no longer a part of the Overland route. Now a secondary line, it remained active as a feeder for local freight, mail, and passenger connections to Oakland, San Jose, Sacramento, and the Central Valley.

Good land in the San Joaquin Valley was available from the government at reasonable prices before the SP was built. Former Confederate soldiers squatted on the lands, never bothering to formally purchase it. They assumed they could pay the government rate of $2.50 per acre for the unimproved land once they had some income. The SP was a land-grant railroad, and clear titles were based on the precedent of McLaughlin's earlier claims. Ownership had to be demonstrated from before the charter date for the SP charter to be recognized. Agents were sent to demand the settlers buy the un-surveyed land for four to ten times the original government rate, pay rent at an exorbitant fee, or face eviction. U.S. Marshals arrived with railroad agents to enforce the evictions and were met by armed settlers. Gunfire broke out and eight were killed. The courts, with judges appointed by Stanford, ruled for the railroad in most of the cases subsequently litigated. The incident, which occurred near Hanford, California, became known as the Mussel Slough Tragedy.[24]

In their attempt to improve railroad business, the major trunk lines brought in settlers from Europe on their own ships and special trains. The cars on the train were little better than cattle cars and had armed guards. The railroad gave the settlers grubstake loans and sold them property to farm. Then they set freight rates sufficiently high that a fraction of the farms would fail each year. The failed farms were repossessed then resold, often several times over. The railroad was necessary to bring in commodities and transport their products to market. Although the railroad supported development, its monopolistic practices and political control generated considerable public animosity.

Before standardized times, every town had its own clock. Clocks were based on solar noon, when the sun reached the highest point in the sky. Railroads usually adopted the solar time of their headquarter town, synchronized across its system by telegraph. Railroad time often differed from local time, especially for east–west running railroads. This led to confusion between the locals and the railroad and occasionally caused collisions of trains operating on different clocks. A railroad time convention in 1883 adopted a system of times based on the central meridians of four zones across the country. This ensured that no town's time would differ more than a half hour from local solar time. The CP reset its standard for the 120th meridian, which was ten minutes ahead of time at its San Francisco headquarters on November 1, 1884.[25] Standard railroad times were adopted by all railroads. Despite some towns protesting that its residents would have to eat, sleep, and work by railroad time, the standard was eventually adopted by the nation in 1918.

Stanford did not agree with Huntington's preferred candidate for a senate seat from California. Using his immense fortune and mobilizing his political cronies, Stanford won the seat for himself.

Huntington never forgot and begrudged Stanford's 1861 election as president of the CP. He was further incensed by Stanford's politicking for his own benefit rather than the interest of the railroad. The election of Stanford to the Senate against Huntington's own candidate was the last straw. Huntington reaped his vengeance by forcing Stanford from his position with the railroad in April 1890. The public was particularly angered by Huntington's takeover.

George Pullman created the Pullman Palace cars and a line of sleeping cars that became ubiquitous across the nation. He built a company town called Pullman, Illinois (now part of Chicago), where he required his employees to live but charged rents barely below the substance wages of those who constructed his cars.

The Panic of 1893 led to an economic depression that ended in 1897 and was the worst since the inception of the nation. In response, Pullman reduced the wages of his employees below substance levels. The depression caused an explosion of long-brewing labor unrest. Eugene Debs merged together brotherhoods of engineers, firemen, brakemen, and others into the American Railroad Union (ARU). The Pullman workers declared a strike and the ARU supported the strike by initiating a boycott of all Pullman sleeping cars.

When an SP trainman refused to move a Pullman car in Sacramento, he was promptly fired. Within days, SP crews refused to move Pullman cars. Long-distance passenger trains carrying Pullman cars were all halted, including the Overland Limited.

Some cars, even trains, were left blocking main lines. A scab engineer was killed when his locomotive encountered a sabotaged rail and was sent tumbling down an embankment. Just days later, the troops broke the strike, and the strike leaders were fired. They were blacklisted from employment on any railroad by having their service records watermarked with a crane with a broken neck.[26]

Huntington had created a railroad monopoly throughout California. The SP monopoly created great wealth and power for the Associates. They took control of the court, the politics, and banks. William Randolph Hearst, critical of Huntington's fingers in every pie and ruthless business practices, characterized him as an octopus. The approbation stuck and later was the inspiration for Frank Norris's novel, *The Octopus*, which was based on actual practices of the Associates and culminating in the Mussel Slough Tragedy.

In typical fashion, Huntington acquired controlling interest in each of the acquired railroads, eventually sweeping them into the octopus of the SP system.[27] The San Francisco press continued to characterize him as a money-grubbing octopus. The renewed approbation foreshadowed the national discontent with railroad practices.

Huntington, in his personal effort to increase his wealth, took control of the Chesapeake and Ohio Railroad. He did not inform the other Associates until the deal was completed. He built a shipyard at Newport News, Virginia, to provide ships to connect his rail lines to New York.[28] In 1894, Huntington controlled the Panama Railroad and was instrumental in creating the New Panama Canal Company.[29]

Overweight and in ill health, Stanford succumbed on January 20, 1893, leaving only Huntington the remaining Associate.[30]

Collis Huntington, the iron-fisted president of both the Central Pacific and Southern Pacific railroads, was the last of the Big Four. He controlled the separate CP and SP boards and those of all the many railroads he acquired. His monopolistic actions continued to raise the ire of the public. He was highly competitive and even feared on Wall Street.

The economy turned around after the depression of 1893–97. Banker Henry Morgenthau noted that the decade after the depression was the

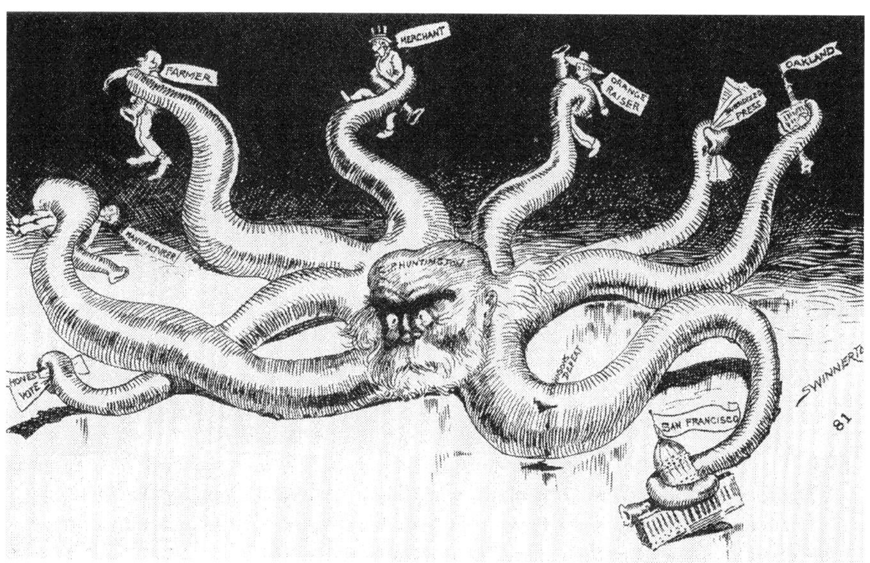

Collis Huntington depicted as an octopus. Drawn by James Swinnerton and published by Hearst. (*Bancroft Library*)

period of greatest expansion of American business.[31] This initiated the final era of competitive railroad construction. It also became a major era of railroad stock manipulation, takeovers, and mergers. Many tycoons were forced out while a few built great monopolies. Much of the building was of lines parallel to those existing. This was to reduce competitors' income, force down the value of their stock, and then take them over.

This not only elevated competition between Wall Street railroad moguls. Other competition began with the emergence of new forms of transportation.

In the early years of the twentieth century, the railroads preferentially encouraged industrial developments, especially those that would regularly utilize carload freight at their own loading docks. The railroads often underwrote the cost of adding a spur track to service those customers promising significant business.

The post-depression period also became the start of significant technical upgrading of existing railroads. The major railroads all undertook efforts to reduce curvature and grades, as well as increasing the weight capacity of rails and bridges. This allowed for longer, faster trains of heavier cars and pulled by larger locomotives.

Huntington's fight to maintain ownership of the CP prevented him from making upgrades, except as necessary. The CP line was not upgraded to a first-class railroad and became a bottleneck for UP traffic to the Bay Area. The old WP / CP through Livermore, being a secondary line, received only the replacement of wooden covered bridges with steel but no major right-of-way improvements. The sharp curves and steep grades of the line remained largely as they were built in the 1860s.

After the depression and with the CP's thirty-year federal construction bonds coming due, Huntington claimed the CP could not raise sufficient funds to pay the debt. Seeking help from congressional "friends," he sought a bill relieving the CP of the bond debt. With Stanford gone, the California politicians and press revolted against Huntington's bill. Hearst's reporter, Ambrose Bierce, exposed the lies and misinformation being presented to Congress by Huntington. The bill was defeated.

The SP was entirely Huntington's transcontinental railroad on a southern route, the Sunset Route, bypassing Donner Pass. It became profitable serving both Northern and Southern California. He redirected traffic from the CP route to the SP route and deferred maintenance, attempting to make the CP economics look dire. He again put the CP on the market to no avail, at least under his terms.

Redirecting the traffic also made the SP more profitable. An arrangement with the government to pay back the bonds in full made Huntington's highly profitable SP responsible for paying off the CP bonds in ten years.

The arrangement effectively leased the CP to the SP for no rent other than the repayment of the bonds to the government.[32] Thereafter the CP was operated and considered part of the SP commencing on July 1, 1892, after the CP-SP deal was finalized.[33] The CP name on stations, cars, and timetables quickly disappeared. The lines from Oakland to Sacramento was CP's Western Division and became SP's Western Division. Unofficially, the CP became a part of the SP but remained a separate company until they were actually merged in 1959.

Huntington, through his clever, often manipulative financial dealings, managed to keep full control of the SP empire until his death in 1900. Huntington did take help from a newcomer, Edward Harriman.

Harriman took over the SP, by buying out the stock willed to Huntington's wife and nephew. He had previously taken over the UP after its bankruptcy during the depression and rehabilitated it to profitability. Owning both the SP and UP made Harriman the principal owner of the largest railroad empire in the nation with a monopoly serving Northern California and the Bay Area.

Harriman significantly improved the public opinion of the railroad when he personally rushed to Oakland from New York after the 1906 earthquake. He then spent two weeks directing all the services of the railroad in the recovery. Services included using all ferries to help evacuate San Francisco, as well as transporting those injured to hospitals for treatment. All the services provided by the railroad were without charge.[34]

Huntington and later Harriman were most concerned with potential competition of parallel lines breaking their monopoly. Harriman, looking to limit the ability of the several proposed new railroads from coming across the Altamont, demanded the full 400-foot right-of-way as granted by the Pacific Railroad Act. Ranchers across the Altamont and through the valley had for years recognized a 100-foot right-of-way. They were incensed when they were required to pay rent for the use of the additional land.[35]

Most railroad moguls, including Gould, Vanderbilt, and Huntington, knew little, nor cared about actual operations of their companies. Their goals were to increase their own wealth through their stock manipulations. Harriman, a master stock manipulator, also understood railroad operations. He improved his railroad companies to be well run and profitable.[36]

Harriman was able to clear the residual debt to the government for the original CP construction bonds. He pushed to bring his railroads to modern standards and make them competitive in order to increase freight and passenger services. He had reworked the neglected CP and SP into efficient, well-managed, well-run, and profitable railroads. He began operating the CP, SP, and UP as one and began the process of merging them into one railroad. However, the strict policies featured in *The Octopus* continued.[37] The strong management team and Edward Harriman's policies persisted after Harriman died.[38]

Several lines were initially chartered through the valley, although none were built. The most ambitious proposal was the California & Nevada RR.[39] It was chartered and surveyed in 1881 to build a narrow-gauge line from Oakland, through the hills via the San Ramon Valley, to the Livermore Coal Mines. They proposed building a tunnel to Corral Hollow. They intended to build across the Sierra by way of Sonora to tap the rich silver deposits in Bodie. Local farmers hoped that the narrow gauge would compete with the CP to reduce freight rates. After nearly two decades, the railroad had constructed only 20 miles of track but had acquired valuable bayfront access near the Shell Mound in Berkeley.

The Atchison, Topeka, and Santa Fe (referred to as the Santa Fe) purchased the California & Nevada. They were rumored to be planning a line into the Bay Area via Livermore.[40] The Santa Fe was not interested in the chartered route but rather valuable waterfront property. The line bypassed Livermore. It was built via Stockton, across northern Contra Costa County, and through Franklyn Canyon. The Santa Fe line opened to Richmond and Berkeley in 1904. It was the first to break the SP monopoly into Northern California by creating the third transcontinental route to the Bay Area.

The Alameda and San Joaquin Valley Railroad (A&SJ) was incorporated in 1895 by a San Francisco group headed by John Treadwell, Walter J. Bartnett, and J. Dalzell Brown.[41] It was chartered to carry coal from Corral Hollow to Stockton. A proposed second phase was to bring coal to Oakland or Alameda via a tunnel from Corral Hollow to Livermore. The proposal also raised considerable local hopes for competition with the SP.[42] The railroad opened to Stockton in 1896 but the tunnel and line through Livermore were never built.

Gould took control of the UP after the 1873 recession. San Francisco Bay was still the major port in California and Gould wanted into the business and knocked down the SP. He took control of railroads into Denver and the nascent Denver and Rio Grande. He planned to build out the Rio Grande to Salt Lake City then acquire the CP. He was initially thwarted by Huntington's success in surviving the 1893 stock market crash, whereas the UP again succumbed into bankruptcy. This exacerbated the competition between Gould and Huntington, which lasted the rest of their lives and beyond. Gould began a secretive effort to build a railroad parallel to the CP to hopefully steal its business and merge his empire into a transcontinental. He died before his project was completed but his son George, pushed it forward.

George Gould and Harriman both sat on the boards of each other's railroads. Although on the surface their relationship appeared amicable, they were in fact fierce Wall Street competitors. Harriman was consolidating his control of the SP & UP to the Bay Area via the CP. Jay Gould acquired railroads connecting from the Atlantic coast to Denver. He then secretly bought a controlling interest in the Rio Grande, which brought his lines to Salt Lake City. All George Gould needed to complete his father's dream of a transcontinental railroad was a line from Salt Lake City to California and San Francisco Bay waterfront access.[43]

Bartnett and Brown, officers of the A&SJ, broadened their goal to extend the coal line not only from Corral Hollow to San Francisco but to Salt Lake City, as well. Bartnett secretly met with George Gould and agreed to form a company to meet their common goals. The Western Pacific Railway (WPRY), with Bartnett as president, was incorporated in California on March 3, 1903.[44] George Gould was the major stockholder, but his participation was kept secret. The WPRY was really a Wall Street pawn in the chess match between the New York railroad moguls, Jay and George Gould, and Harriman. The A&SJ was secretly purchased by the WPRY that July.

Later it was announced that David Moffat, president of the Gould's Rio Grande, would financially back the WPRY. Brown also incorporated the Western Pacific Construction Company in Nevada, following the practice of the CP and UP to create a privately owned construction and money laundering company.

Both the A&SJ and WPRY separately chartered small railways to ostensibly service mining interests in the vicinity of Beckwourth Pass in the Sierra Nevada range. Confrontations between construction crews of the mining railroads were featured in the press. The confrontations were intended to obscure the fact of common ownership and the real goal of Beckwourth Pass as the Sierra crossing for a transcontinental railroad. Surveyors from both roads continued staking out their routes up the Feather River and across Nevada.[45]

Gould finally admitted his involvement in the WPRY and resigned from Harriman's boards. Harriman also resigned from the Rio Grande board. Vowing to stop the WPRY, Harriman denied the Rio Grande a connection to the West Coast via the CP by blocking an interchange at Ogden. He then apparently charged the WPRY exorbitant rates for shipment of construction materials via the UP&SP.[46]

Theodore Roosevelt's justice department sued Harriman's railroad holding company, Northern Securities Company, to undo the UP, SP merger. Roosevelt championed amending the Interstate Commerce Commission's (ICC) Charter of 1887 and giving the Sherman Antitrust Act of 1890 some teeth to prevent the consolidation of railroads into monopolies.[47] After years of litigation, the United States Supreme Court interpreted the acts to protect trade and commerce against unlawful restraints and monopolies.[48] The court finally forced the breakup of the SP and UP in 1913.[49] UP continued to fight for ownership of the CP which was still formally a separate company, until it was settled in favor of the SP.[50]

Subsequently, public animosity toward the railroads shifted federal support to paved highways, later airports, eventually breaking the rail monopoly on transportation. Despite Roosevelt's recognition of the foolishness of the Gilded Age's destructive competition, the Wall Street games continued until Roosevelt's policies took effect.

The Pacific Railroad Act gave the railroads the right to take unclaimed land and McLaughlin with the court's acts to take land from the land grant *rancheros*. There was limited development in the valley at that time and property owners saw the WPRY as potentially increasing their land value. The acquisition of the WPRY right of way across the settled town of Livermore was a completely different process than the original WP. Mendenhall's original gift to the WP included little more than a formal surveyed property description. WPRY asked the town for a franchise to construct and operate a railway across a stated route along Oak Street.[51] The city's WPRY franchise included all the town rules and railroad conditions as they had evolved through the years. Livermore Ordinance 37 granting the franchise was unanimously adopted by the trustees.[52]

The WPRY initially announced that its route would follow the coal road track and survey. A 7,000-foot tunnel was planned from Corral Hollow to Livermore.[53] Test borings revealed much fractured rock and other hazards, which would significantly drive up the cost of the tunnel. Consequently, the WPRY announced a revised route over the Altamont, which directly paralleled the CP line.[54] The new route climbed above the CP, so no summit tunnel was required, only a deep cut. WPRY tracks crossed the SP in three places around Livermore, at Trevarno and twice on the Altamont.

The WPRY had major technical advantages which enhanced long-distance freight service. Railroad construction practices after 1900 were significantly different from those in the 1860s. Grades and curvatures were reduced, allowing heavier trains at higher speeds. The Beckwourth Pass over the Sierra was 2,000 feet lower than Donner, making the crossing easier, especially in the winter. Gould was able to prevail in a battle with SP over waterfront access in Oakland. The WPRY was completed and went into service in 1910.

The WPRY was late in the game into the Bay Area after the CP, SP, and Santa Fe. It became the seventh and last of the transcontinental railroads constructed. Its gala opening featured the fancy Spanish Mission-styled

Livermore Depot, designed by architect W. H. Mohr. The apparently grand welcome for the new line was largely a response to the years of ruinously high freight rates and big corporation policies of the SP. The local populace looked forward to reduced freight rates and better service, which they anticipated the new line would bring.

The WPRY was the result of personal goals, unregulated competition, and animosities among the robber barons at the height of the railroad building boom at the dawn of the twentieth century. The result was a parallel line ostensibly offering the same services as the SP. The hopes of Livermore's residents, farmers, and ranchers were dashed when WPRY fees and practices were the same as the SP's.

The new WPRY never served the local interests, as did the SP. The WPRY line was a transcontinental mainline with almost no feeder lines; its service was entirely based on long-distance freight. Most existing local freight stayed with the SP. Initially with no freight traffic from Livermore, the WPRY was competitive only for new long-term commercial customers.

Passenger services required by the government were scheduled primarily for long-distance passengers. For the most part, it consisted of a through train with connections to the Rio Grande and Burlington for service to Chicago. A secondary train served mostly as a shuttle for crews.

Through fares for either railroad were identical. Both railroads offered reduced fares for special events, such as a picnic in Niles Canyon (CP/SP), a Druid Festival in San Francisco (CP/SP), a trip to the Feather River Canyon (WPRY), and long-distance summer specials.

The physical trackage and destinations of the WPRY were largely parallel to the CP; the level and quality of passenger service was clearly not. Most passenger service was, at best, slow and bare bones, despite fancy names such as the *Feather River Express*, *Chicago Express*, or the *Exposition Flyer*. Trains were renamed for new enticements, such as the Chicago Exposition, perhaps with an added amenity. The WPRY ran mostly just two and, rarely, three passenger trains a day each way; the SP had more stopping in Livermore. Local service on the WPRY was more limited than the original WP services of forty years earlier. The WPRY generally offered only one through train a day from Oakland to Salt Lake. Secondary trains often terminated at Oroville.

Schedules were rarely useful for Livermore passengers. Even though all the WPRY trains were relatively long distance, the secondary trains did not carry any food service, whereas the longer-distance SP trains carried at least an all-day lunch car, which provided café service. The top-of-the-line SP service included elegant dining cars with reasonable prices. About the only conveniences on the WPRY secondary trains were smoking and non-smoking cars.

The finances of the WPRY reached the point where advances from private stockholders could no longer cover the company's debts. It fell into receivership in 1915 and was sold in foreclosure to a consortium of the debt holders. Operations continued, although only a word in the name was changed from Railway to Railroad to preserve its identity. The company was converted to a publicly owned corporation and then challenged with eleven years of litigation. The WPRY was an economic failure. Service was considerably poorer than the SP. Freight rates and passenger fares were identical with the SP and did not create competition.

The development and popularization of automobiles was initially ignored by the railroads as insignificant competition. They were federally required to provide local service, although they were always operated at a loss. The railroads sought to profit from the new automobile craze by delivering the large quantities of fuel by rail tank car.

WPRY installed short spur sidings to service the depots of Union Oil and Standard Oil of California. They were located on opposite sides of the main track. just east of the town charter line. Richfield Oil built a depot in the SP station site at O Street within the downtown loop siding.[55]

Initially, rail crossings were privately and informally created as needed locally. They were usually just dirt filling between and ramping on either side of the rails. Rail crossings were and continue to be accident prone. Most horses, unless properly trained, would rear, buck, or bolt at the sound of the steam. Other accidents occurred when drivers failed to yield to an oncoming train, or when rain turned the crossing to mud, causing wagons to get stuck. These accidents rarely caused much damage to the train, so they were mostly ignored by the railroad. In most cases, the crossings were built privately after the railroad, allowing the railroad to claim absolute right-of-way and no responsibility. Eventually, it became the responsibility of the town to protect the crossings. The growth of automobile traffic increased the number and especially more serious crossing accidents.

Upgraded crossings had wooden planks over stringers nailed to the ties below. The planks were level with the top of the rail and made a very distinctive sound when they were crossed by a wagon or vehicle. Approved crossings were those jointly agreed to by the town council and the railroad.

Poor visibility made the crossing at Lizzie Street particularly dangerous. The town clerk was directed to correspond with the railroad authorities and see whether they would hire a flagman to protect the crossing. The railroad refused as the town was responsible for the safety of its streets and that crossing was built after the railroad. A flagman was eventually hired by the town after the street was paved.

Initially, the only safety apparatus was the locomotive's steam whistle. The flagman protected the Lizzie Street SP crossing for seven years until an automated signal was installed.[56] Warning signals were installed at major crossings; at first these were automated flashing lights or bells. The automatic flagman, the so-called wigwag, became the major crossing safety apparatus for half of the twentieth century. The wigwag had a steel target on a pendulum with a red light in the center. An approaching train triggered the pendulum to swing, turning on the red light and ringing a bell.

Protecting crossings with wigwags commenced immediately after World War I and continued for years. SP allowed the city to install wigwags across its yard tracks. Crossings with a wigwag or a crossbuck with flashing lights were considered "protected." However, nothing prevented vehicles from passing them. Crossing guards which lowered an arm across the lane(s) of traffic were not installed in Livermore until the 1960s.

In several cases, it took a deadly accident at a crossing to get the town council and railroad to install safety apparatus. Although the council helped defray the cost of an installation, the railroad became responsible for its maintenance.

Failure of a safety device created a liability for the railroad. Some crossings remained unprotected. An unprotected crossing had, at most,

This Southern Pacific photo, looking north on Livermore Avenue *circa* 1925, shows the CP/SP crossing at Livermore Avenue, with a wigwag signal in the middle of the street. The WPRY crossing and wigwag is seen in the distance. The buildings in the first block on the left are today's Blacksmith Square. The derelict two-story building across Railroad Avenue was the Farmers Union. (*Union Pacific Museum*)

a crossbuck with the words "RAILROAD CROSSING" and occasionally "STOP LOOK LISTEN."

Automated signals did not eliminate crossing accidents, especially by those ignoring the signal. The California Railroad Commission announced it would make every effort to abolish grade crossings to prevent accidents that were occurring daily.[57] The Livermore Police were tasked to enforce the portion of the National Traffic and Motor Vehicle Safety Act passed in 1931 that required all vehicles to stop at unprotected crossings or at a protected crossing when a warning signal was activated.

The SP requested that the town install a pair of wigwags for the new crossing at L Street.[58] An unofficial crossing existed at L Street for decades but was finally approved. The town engineer initially rejected the request because he wanted the depot moved to a location between L Street and Livermore Avenue so that trains would not block the crossing. A new water tank and plumbing eliminated the need for trains to block the crossing while taking on water. At the same time, the passing siding was extended to allow switching of cars while not blocking either the main track or the L Street crossing. Complaints of the unofficial L Street crossing of the SP being blocked continued even after the completion of the extended siding, new tank and water system. The L Street crossing became official when the SP allowed the city to install safety apparatus. The city asked SP to extend K Street but was immediately rebuffed by the railroad.[59]

The WPRY had the opposite crossing issues with the city. When built, the railroad was required to provide a crossing at every platted street it crossed. The railroad's continuing interest was in reducing as many crossings as possible and requiring grade separations for any new ones. When the WPRY was constructed, the only two crossings of the SP from the Northern Addition to downtown were East First Street crossing and Livermore Avenue crossing. All the other north–south streets which crossed the WPRY were blocked at Railroad Avenue.

The year 1916 marked a turning point in national railroad building. Track on the ground peaked at 254,037 miles and declined every year thereafter. At the same time, continued public ill will festered, with ICC approval of requests for ticket and freight rate increases, as well as abandonment of unprofitable lines.[60] At that time, most passenger service and freight were still dominated by the railroads. The country had not yet been directly involved in the war in Europe, the government was already responding to the pressures on the transportation system.

During World War I, the government nationalized the railroads creating the United States Railroad Administration (USRA) to operate them. The goal was to unify railroad operations for the war effort and set aside competitive limitations. The USRA instituted major changes in the rail industry.[61] Freight rates were standardized on a per-mile basis rather than the highest the traffic would bear. Work rules were standardized, including an eight-hour day. Trackage rights were implemented such that any train could use the best available track and route, independent of what railroad the track belonged to.

Priorities were given to troop trains and military equipment. The USRA standardized equipment. Previously every railroad custom designed to suit their needs. Policies favored war production.

The SP and WPRY were operated as one railroad under the USRA but were again independent competitors afterwards.[62] The railroads were returned to their original owners in 1920, but many of the changes initiated by the USRA remained in practice. Although the USRA effectively eliminated inequities, including the usurious freight rates and the free passes, it was too late to reverse the public opinion and lack of support for the railroads.

The railroads financially benefited from the nationalization, despite the imposed changes. The financial boost finally lifted the WPRY out of its first bankruptcy and reorganization. The mid-1920s was a period when the railroads invested their profits accumulated during the war.

The WPRY, looking to increase its business, joined with the Great Northern (GN) to create a sixth transcontinental route into the Bay Area. At that time, GN was a transcontinental between Saint Paul, Minnesota, Portland, Oregon, and Seattle, Washington. It was the only transcontinental built entirely without government support.[63]

With San Francisco Bay still the predominant port on the West Coast, GN desired access via the WPRY. Both railroads needed additional business to fend off competition. Working jointly, the WPRY built north from Keddie, in Plumas County, California, while GN built south from its spur to Klamath Falls, Oregon. They met at Bieber, California, east of Mt. Shasta, two years later, opening what they called the Inside Gateway.[64] The line also connected to several feeder roads bringing in lumber shipments.

SP's post-war station improvement program included spending $20,000 to upgrade its crossings through town. The railroad had, at that time, six crossings, only three over the main tracks and three over sidings. SP claimed the crossings would be the smoothest and most durable of any in the state.[65] SP also worked to modernize and upgrade station infrastructure. The depot office was enlarged, and a ladies' dressing room was added in the waiting area.[66] The temporary wooden water tank hurriedly erected after the 1906 earthquake was replaced by a modern steel tank in 1923.[67] The new tank was south of the tracks and west of L Street. It fed standpipes underground so that trains no longer had to block L Street while taking on water. Station Agent Heaney commented that there were six SP passenger train stops a day that blocked the L Street crossing for only about two minutes each. He thus claimed crossing traffic was delayed only about twelve minutes a day.[68] This alleviated many complaints about the blocked crossing and even quieted suggestions of moving the depot.

Station Agent Heaney reported that twenty-six SP employees at Livermore were annually paid nearly $44,000 in 1928. They included eight station employees, one signalman, six switching crew, two engine watchmen, and nine section men.[69]

The development of significantly larger locomotives required a turntable too long for the available space at the Livermore station. The old turntable and engine house were removed, and an additional spur was laid south of the main track in 1924 to improve switching of cars to customers.[70] A steam locomotive service facility remained; however, locomotives had to be turned elsewhere. The passing siding was reconfigured to extend from Trevarno nearly to Murrieta. It was mainly to speed through freight while providing additional trackage for switching.[71] Previously, the siding looped north of the old water tank and was straightened when the new tank was installed on the south side of the main track. The SP also started expanding their charter by developing their own bus and trucking companies.

The WPRY continued trying to compete by eliminating losing services. Parallel continued to challenge the railroad. The WPRY announced cutbacks in passenger service for its premier trains.[72] It built a long spur line from Niles to San Jose more than half a century after the CP began service to that city.[73] It abandoned the old coal road to Tesla as the mines had shut down.[74]

The 1929 Stock Market Crash ended railroad growth and initiated a retrenchment that would last for the next fifty years.

6

CHANGE

Significant political changes, diversified transportation, prohibition, and women's suffrage altered local ways of life in the first years of the twentieth century.

Livermore's population was essentially stable around 2,000 at the turn of the century. The town's population mostly provided the shops and services that supported the farmers and ranchers throughout the valley. Growth of the town was limited and a significant number of unbuilt lots remained.

Livermore businesses were not significantly affected by the 1890s depression. Export of agricultural products continued as before. Wine, farm, ranch, and warehouse business continued unabated. There was minimal, if any Wall Street investment by the town's population. Mining and manufacturing remained small because of a limited working population.

The post-depression boom created inflation, which doubled the cost of living through the next twenty years. Increased farm products prices largely offset the cost-of-living rise.[1] Whenever Chinese workers were hired, there was an uproar before the trustees and in the newspapers. They claimed those jobs needed to be reserved for white people.

Livermore prospered and the state-funded organization of a local unit of the National Guard. The unit was Company I, Fifth Infantry of the California National Guard, which officially existed from 1900 to 1917 and had up to 414 members. The guard was headquartered at the Sweeney Opera House. The unit served some interesting and important duties. Early on, the company was invited to march in the parade welcoming President Teddy Roosevelt to San Francisco. The celebrations ran late, and the company missed the last train home for the day.

They wound up having to sleep on the floor at the First Regiment Armory and then made it home the next morning.[2] The company served in San Francisco with the recovery effort after the 1906 earthquake. The company's first action was on the Mexican border. Later it was merged with Company A in 1917 and integrated into the 40th Division of 159th Infantry.[3] Eight members of the "Old Company" were lost in Europe during World War I.[4] A memorial to the members lost in the war was constructed adjacent to the library in Carnegie Park.[5]

Livermore was still the railroad center of the valley at the turn of the century. The railroad handled nearly all the transport of products, people, mail, and materials between towns, near and far. Horse and wagon were used to transport people and material to and from the train station and around town. Station agents after the retirement of Mitchel were all SP, having no interaction with the town other than railroad business.

The post-recession boom initiated the most intense Wall Street trading and competition amongst railroad owners. The swashbuckling robber-baron Jay Gould undertook to build a transcontinental into the bay area to compete with the Southern Pacific (SP). He disliked Huntington and named his railroad the Western Pacific Railroad (WPRY) just for spite.

Station Agent John L. Mitchel retired in 1903. He was the agent from the earliest days of both the town and the railroad and an important and respected member of the community. The station agent's role was a highly responsible one and often provided a stepping stone to higher authority.

Company I members in 1904. (*Livermore Heritage Guild*)

Those who came after Mitchel were purely railroad men. Some barely lasted a year in the job, though none longer than Mitchel.

William Barrow Bayley was Livermore's station agent from 1905 to 1913. His granddaughter, Dottie Eberly, shared the detail that Bayley's children were born in the depot.[6] He oversaw Harriman's modernization efforts and reported additional freight traffic requiring a second helper locomotive to be based in Livermore. He was promoted to become a more prestigious and higher-paid agent in Oakland and retired in 1929.[7]

Meetings were conducted advocating women's suffrage.[8] There was only limited attendance, and nothing came of them. The Ladies League of Progress did not support female suffrage amendment to state constitution as they were formed to support the library.[9] A California election giving women the right to vote was narrowly approved by voters across the state with 50.7 percent support.

A large crowd came out to greet President William McKinley's train when he passed through town in 1901. The crowd indicated the local interest in national politics. The president's wife was ailing, so he had cut short his national tour and was rushing home. The size of the crowd convinced the president to make a brief whistle-stop to wave to the crowd and shake a few hands without leaving the train.[10] Sadly, McKinley was assassinated just two weeks later, thrusting Theodore Roosevelt into the White House.

President McKinley on the train stopped in Livermore. (*Livermore Heritage Guild*)

Teddy Roosevelt's presidency effectively marked the time when the railroads began to lose their place as the dominant mode of transportation in the nation. Edward Harriman's acquisition of the SP, the retirement of Station Agent Mitchel, Roosevelt's trust-busting policies and continued Wall Street trading wars, arbitrary freight rates and passenger fares, building parallel lines, and unreasonable services all increased public animosity. The emergence of competitive modes of transportation fostered major changes in Livermore's relationship with the railroads.

Fredrick Mally opened a shoe repair business in Laddsville before Livermore was formed. His business was burned out in the 1871 fire, and he started a new business in Livermore. He built a store on the south side of First Street between J and K streets where he expanded to selling fancy goods.[11] His family lived in the building, and there were a couple of extra rooms that were rented to roomers. Fred Mally bought into the Livermore Restaurant Saloon that became the Grill Annex and was later renamed Mally's Grill and Cocktail Lounge in 1902. His son, Clarence, took over the business after his father's death.

The Palace Hotel, formerly Anton Bardellini's Washington Hotel, was built in 1875. Located next door to the grill, the hotel was previously bought by the Mally family.[12] The grill became well known in the first half of the twentieth century for its special events as well as good food, low prices, and as a destination restaurant for people coming by train from Oakland and San Francisco.[13] Dinner was only 50 cents, and regulars could buy a twenty-meal ticket for $5.[14] The name was changed to Mally's Grill and Coffee Shop during Prohibition.

Mally's Hotel and Grill. (*Livermore Heritage Guild*)

The Fourth of July committee had an excess of funds in 1904. They decided to erect a flagpole in Mill Square at the corner of Lizzy and First streets. The Douglas fir pole was 126 feet tall and came from a ship builder in Oakland. The railroad could not ship the pole because it was too long for three or four flat cars to round the curves. An eight-mule team pulling timber wagons took two days to haul it up Dublin Canyon. Charles Lefever raised the flagpole.[15] It was in place and celebrated the following September.[16] The flagpole was dedicated at a ceremony on admission day in 1905 and served for ninety-nine years.

The town council purchased the two-story former Livermore Valley Bank building on the southeast corner of First and McLeod streets in 1905. A single-story fire house was constructed alongside. The building was modernized, surfaced with stucco, and was the town hall and then city hall for nearly fifty years and is still a feature of downtown.[17]

John Sweeney built the Sweeney Opera House on the southwest corner of McLeod and first streets in 1904.[18] It was called an opera house because a twenty-year-old ordinance forbid "dance halls or houses of ill fame." Despite its name, it was intended to be and was mostly used as a dance hall. It opened with the Fireman's Ball given by the Livermore Concert Band and also hosted the annual July Fourth Ball.[19,20]

The main hall with a balcony could seat 800 attendees. Other dances and major school events were conducted there. It was the largest hall in Alameda County and hosted traveling vaudeville, opera, music and theatrical productions. The National Guard unit's weekly drills occurred on the main floor and its headquarters was in a second-story office. The hall was destroyed by fire just after World War II.[21]

Traditional balls became too costly and began to fade for entertainment and fundraising after the turn of the century. A chapter of the first international service club, the Fraternal Order of Eagles, was formed in Livermore and celebrated with a ball in 1904.[22,23] Some of the traditional balls continued to celebrate holidays and organizations until shortly after World War I. Non-profit social dances largely replaced the expensive balls. A local post of the American Legion was formed shortly after World War I.[24] They began a series of dances for the veterans and soldiers.

Movies became an increasingly popular form of entertainment. The first movie shown in town was at the Foresters Ball in the Farmers' Union in 1902. A nickelodeon opened in the Brewery Building on the south side of First Street between J and K streets in 1908. Sweeney's Opera House also started showing movies. The Bell Theatre initially opened in 1909 on Second and J streets and then moved into the Schenone building when it was completed in 1913.[25,26] The Bell Theatre was sold and its name changed to the Livermore Theater, then the California Theater. The silent

The Bell Theatre in the newly completed Schenone building. (*Livermore Heritage Guild*)

movies generally had live piano or organ accompaniment until talkies were introduced.[27] A fire closed the theater which was rebuilt and then opened as the State Theater with upgraded sound.[28] The State Theater was a fixture in downtown until the Vine Cinema was opened in 1956.[29]

Radio broadcasting became a popular source of news and entertainment in the early 1920s. Stations in the Bay Area could be received in Livermore. A radio shop was opened on First Street then other shops began to sell radios. Some complained of dead spots where certain stations could not be heard.[30] Gardella's Jazz Orchestra played on Oakland radio station KLX in 1924.[31]

Sports teams continued expanding to mostly baseball and basketball. Teams represented local supporting organizations or the schools and several competed regionally.

Motoring took hold from the beginning of the twentieth century. The first local article was published in the *Herald* in 1899 and read, "It is rumored the Valley is soon to have an auto. Mrs. Hearst is said to have purchased one on her recent visit to Paris. If true, ours will be the first rural community in the state to have one of these marvelous vehicles."[32]

Former Livermore resident W. L. Elliot made a pioneering long-distance auto trip driving from San Francisco to Bakersfield over several days. Leaving San Francisco at noon, he arrived in Livermore for his first night at 7:30 p.m. He was impressed with the quality of the roads in the valley and claimed they allowed him to reach 25 mph. He received considerable local interest and took Judge Taylor for a ride.[33] The Locomobile Company of the Pacific demonstrated its gasoline-heated, steam-powered vehicle in Livermore. Bicycle dealer Henry R. Crane became the Locomobile agent in Livermore.[34] Steam-driven cars caused horses to panic and bolt along the only road from the Bay Area to the Central Valley through Livermore.[35]

Dr. William S. Taylor bought a Haynes-Apperson which in 1903 was the first automobile owned in Livermore. The car took more than ten weeks for delivery as only a few hundred were being constructed each year, and the company was heavily back ordered.[36] Dr. Taylor noted, "No doubt the automobile is practical" for making house calls. It had one of the earliest lightweight, water-cooled gasoline engines designed by Elwood Haynes in 1894. It ran well on city gravel streets; okay in the country but holes occasionally damaged the pneumatic tires. On a good road he could reach 30 mph.[37]

Dr. James Kyle Warner purchased a 10-hp Cadillac through Crane Brothers. He later traded it for a 7-hp Oldsmobile. Though a good machine, the Cadillac was too heavy and found to be ill-adapted for a physician's use.[38] Henry R. Crane built an automobile storehouse and shop on Stevens' lot opposite his cyclery.[39] Norris Dewitt Dutcher rented

Dr. W. S. Taylor in his Haynes-Apperson. He was the first car owner in Livermore. (*Livermore Heritage Guild*)

a former tin shop for a stock of buggies, bicycles, motorcycles, and autos and had an expert mechanic in charge to do general repair work.[40] Crane Brothers became the major early dealership in Livermore representing Oldsmobile, Cadillac, Autocar, Pope-Hartford, Rambler, Marsh, Ford, etc. Crane Brothers sold a California-made motorcycle, the first machine of the kind operated in the valley.[41] Initially, local dealers including Crane and W. H. Taylor ordered cars individually, though by 1914 they were ordering them by full railcar loads.[42]

Growing disenchantment with the railroads encouraged the sale and development of automobiles and the paving of roads. These made local transportation and local delivery of goods quicker and less expensive. Automobiles, trucks, and buses eventually became the major competitors of the railroads. Automotive services expanded as roads were built and paved.

The acquisitions of motor vehicles were of sufficient interest that announcements of local purchases were reported in the newspapers almost every week over several years. In Livermore, auto dealers were established, and blacksmiths became auto repair shops. More automobiles on the streets were accompanied by increasing accidents. Clarence Beck died as a result of an auto accident. It was the first reported fatal accident in Livermore.[43]

A federal act to aid states in the construction of rural post roads was approved in 1916. The act initiated funding for Post Roads, which included roads over which mail was to be carried. The act split the cost of building the roads with the states, and then required the states to maintain them. By the 1930s, automobiles had surpassed the railroads in passenger miles.

Many streets in town continued to be dirt. They were graveled sporadically and slowly funded by adjacent property owners. Roads were watered to keep down dust in the summer and oiled when water was scarce.[44] Streets were being graded to reduce water damage with heavy winter rains. Lizzie and First streets were flooded up to two feet deep on multiple occasions. Automobilists complained about the poor quality of the streets and roads. There was discussion of paving streets as the number of automobiles and editorial support in the newspaper increased.[45] However, little could be done at any one time because of the cost and limited town finances.

The building built by Andrew McLeod in 1882, on the northeast corner of First and Lizzie Streets, is shown during flooding in 1904. The building contained the Bank of Livermore, the offices of the *Livermore Herald* and dentist Dr. S. L. Savage on the second floor and the Masonic Hall on the top floor. Dr. Savage and his family are in the carriage. The building was torn down in 1920 and replaced by the Bank of Italy. (*Livermore Heritage Guild*)

Paving and auto safety became an increasingly important issue for the road and streets committee of the town council. The council considered bitulithic or brick paving.[46] Bitulithic defined a miscellaneous mixture of bitumen and aggregate. The road committee consulted other towns concerning the advantages or disadvantages of the various mixtures they used. They chose the mixture of tar with fine gravel and sand used by Los Angeles.[47] That mixture became known as asphalt. Downtown portions of First Street were paved later that year. Parking lines were painted and stop signs appeared after the downtown streets were paved.[48, 49]

An editorial in the *Livermore Echo* noted:

Numerous violations are reported of the automobile speed limit ordinance, which restricts autos to 10 miles per hour in town, while many go several times this speed. A few arrests of speeding autoists would be a good idea to bring them down to a safe speed, as sooner or later some certain accidents will occur. Motorcyclists have also been riding their noisy machines through town without mufflers, which should be prohibited.[50]

During an especially cold spell, the newspaper noted, "Several local automobilists have learned better than to leave water in the radiators on nights when the temperature is far below freeze as they are something like sieves on the morning after."[51]

The great San Francisco earthquake knocked the tops off the brick chimneys of the Livermore depot, as well as many others in the town. The tops of the depot's chimneys were replaced by stove pipes. The station's water tank was also toppled, causing some localized flooding.[52]

A temporary water tank was rapidly placed on a timber base. The new tank located just west of L Street, like its predecessor, required trains taking water to block the crossing.[53] Despite localized damage, the rail line through Livermore was the only line to remain open into the Bay Area immediately after the earthquake, although a slide in Niles Canyon slowed trains.[54] The station served as the embarkation point for Livermore's National Guard, Company I, to aid San Francisco after the earthquake. The guard unit spent over a month in the fight against the effects of the earthquake and fire. Livermore also became a destination for about 100 refugees fleeing the debacle in San Francisco.[55]

A petition from George Gould's Western Pacific Railway Company, submitted to the Livermore Board of Trustees, asked for a franchise to construct and operate the railway across the town on a stated route along Oak Street. A single protest was heard three weeks later from Mr. Israel Horton, claiming it would destroy his property. Spokesmen for the railroad noted that the proposed route did less damage to private property and was the most feasible of several surveys made by them.[56]

The franchise awarded by the town gave the railroad a right-of-way down the middle of Oak Street. Elsewhere, it had to cross privately owned property. The WPRY angered several locals by usurping resident owners' property by means of condemnation. Their land, farmed or ranched, often provided much of their livelihood. St. Michael Catholic Church fought the acquisition by the WPRY in court over part of their property. The property along east First Street in Laddsville was sold to the church by the Ladd family for $1 in 1881.[57] The church sued the WPRY against its condemnation. It was eventually awarded $500 by the court.[58]

Settlement in Livermore's Northern Addition increased the need for streets to cross the tracks. When the plat of the Northern Addition was registered, there were only two official CP grade crossings: Lizzie (Livermore Avenue) and East First Streets. When the WPRY built across town on Oak Street, they added crossings at east First Street, Junction and North Livermore avenues, as well as I, K, L, M, and N streets. Most WPRY crossings preserved the access to streets within the addition but did not connect across the SP to downtown. A provision of the franchise was that the WPRY was responsible for crossing safety because they were on town property. Complaints of excessive whistling grew with so many close-together crossings on the WPRY. The WPRY through Livermore was built mostly by immigrants from Chili, and most of its work still used horse or mule-drawn equipment. They had a major construction camp and ranch at Trevarno where the Fuse Works was later built.[59]

The WPRY featured a fancy Spanish Mission-styled Livermore Depot, designed by architect W. H. Mohr. The apparently grand welcome for the new line was largely a response to the years of ruinously high freight rates and big corporation policies of the SP. The local populace looked forward to reduced freight rates and better service, which they anticipated the new line would bring. The WPRY ostensibly offered the same services as the SP. The hopes of competitive freight costs for Livermore's residents, farmers, and ranchers were dashed when WPRY fees and practices were the same as the SP's. The new WPRY never served the local interests, and passenger service was considerably poorer than the SP. The schedule was of little use to the community, going east in the morning and west in the afternoon. The local passenger service was mostly intended for crew scheduling, though they did offer specials in attempts to lure passengers. The WPRY was an economic failure. It was reorganized through bankruptcy three times in the next thirty years.

Coast Manufacturing and Supply Company, known as the Fuse Works, made black powder fuses starting in 1913. They made safety fuses for explosives and moved to Livermore from San Leandro. It was located just 2 miles east of town and was served by the SP line at a station called Trevarno.

The Lincoln Highway was conceived in 1912 to be the first automobile road across the nation. It was funded privately and dedicated the following year. After World War I, Brevet Lieutenant Colonel Dwight Eisenhower led a convoy of the Motor Transport Corps across the country on the Lincoln Highway. His concern was the ability to rapidly deploy troops in time of war. Many portions of the highway were still dirt or mud tracks, creating significant problems for the convoy. The challenging expedition took sixty-two days, passing through Livermore before arriving at the West Coast.[60] The paving of the segment of the Lincoln Highway through Livermore marked a major increase of small, local and regional deliveries by truck.[61] Much of the highway eventually became part of U.S. Route 50.

Frank H. Duarte built a service station at L Street along the Lincoln Highway. The garage helped make Livermore a major stop along the highway. Demolition of the garage scheduled by the city was rescinded by negotiation with LHG in the 1970s. It was restored and turned into a museum featuring the early automotive history of the town and the Lincoln Highway.

Gasoline was not refined locally, and large amounts were needed for automobiles. Fuel was initially delivered in barrels. Depots were constructed to receive fuels delivered by rail tank cars. Gasoline and oils

The Duarte Garage opened in 1915. (*Livermore Heritage Guild*)

were then locally trucked to gas stations and other customers. The WPRY installed short spur sidings to service the depots of Union Oil and Standard Oil of California. They were located on opposite sides of the main track just east of the town charter line. Richfield Oil built a depot at O Street within the downtown siding.[62]

Standard Oil built a gas station at the southeast corner of Lizzie and First streets.[63] They sold Red Crown Gasoline at .25 cents a gallon.[64] Gas stations began to proliferate in the next couple of years including ones at L and First Streets, N and First, and East First at the junction with the Lincoln Highway (Portola). Gas price wars erupted between the multitude of stations, with prices plunging to .14 cents a gallon.[65]

The Liberty Bell, on route to San Francisco for the 1915 Panama-Pacific Exposition, made a five-minute whistle-stop in Livermore.[66] The bell was on the open platform of the last car of the SP train and was cheered by an estimated crowd of 2,000 who were serenaded by the Livermore High School Band.[67]

St. Michael's Church, built in 1891, replaced an earlier small church on a site given by Ladd's estate. The church burned to the ground in 1916 after a fire which started in the neighboring lumberyard spread. John "Jack" Jensen, a fireman on the scene, commented, "that was the only one that got away."[68]

The United States Railroad Administration (USRA) operated both the SP and WPRY railroads through Livermore as one during World War I. With the end of the USRA, the Livermore Chamber of Commerce asked the State Railroad Commission to authorize an interconnect between the SP and WPRY to shorten the route for receipt and shipment of goods. Without it, cars from one railroad with business at a loading dock on the other would have to be transferred at an interchange yard, requiring additional fees and mileage.[69] The proposal would effectively have merged freight operations for Livermore. The request was rejected by the railroads.

Livermore was assessed $1,200 as its quota to support the Red Cross during World War I. The Livermore Stockmen's Protective Association under John McGlinchey, president, proposed a rodeo to raise the money. Joseph Concannon was appointed chairman of the planning committee. The event was a success, raising $2,500. They initiated a parade through downtown and a dance. The proprietor of the Bell Movie Theater, G. F. Madsen, filmed the event which became a newsreel shown around the country. The Livermore Stockmen's Rodeo Association was formed the next year. The rodeo and parade continue to be presented annually to the present time.[70]

In recent years, a float in the rodeo parade sponsored by the Lions Club was a miniature calaboose on a flatbed truck. The calaboose was driven around town before the parade. Someone coming to the parade not in cowboy wear, preferably a city councilman, would have his tie cut off and be locked up in the hoosegow for his crime. He was required to make a donation to the parade for bail. If not, he would be paraded through town in the calaboose.[71] Don and Jane Rasmussen first met in the calaboose in 1958 and were married the following year.[72]

The Bank of Italy building was erected in 1921, on the northeast corner of First Street and Livermore Avenue. It became the branch office of the Bank of America from 1957 to 1978. It then served as city hall for a year and was subsequently purchased by the *Independent* newspaper as its office. It is on the National Register of Historic Places.

Gravel quarrying mostly served the railroads before the war. SP opened a quarry at Eliot, 4 miles west of town.[73] Gravel for roads rapidly exceeded the needs of the railroads afterwards. The Kaiser Paving Company opened a gravel quarry south of Stanley Boulevard and West of S Street in 1923.[74] Kaiser's quarry expanded and SP added a spur siding across Stanley to service the pit.[75] Rhodes Jamieson Co. bought the Stoewen Ranch located west of town and opened a quarry two years after Kaiser's opening.[76]

Mining of specialized ores for manganese and chromium picked up before the war. Most significant was magnesite (magnesium oxide), used

Calaboose in the rodeo parade. (*Livermore Heritage Guild*)

in manufacturing fire brick. Rich deposits were found high up on Red and Cedar Mountains just across the Santa Clara County line on Mines Road. Pack mules or horse-drawn wagons were not able to bring the ore down the mountain and to Livermore on Mines Road.[77] Specialized auto trucks had to be built for the task.[78] The dirt, steep, winding, and narrow roads were often not useable in the rainy season forcing limited mining until spring.[79] After the first war, magnesite mining near Livermore increased and became the best producer in the nation.[80] Whereas, the mining of other minerals decreased.

The Livermore Firebrick Company, started in 1910, specialized in magnesite-based firebrick.[81] The plant was specifically built to use the magnesite ore from the local mines. They developed a plant that ran from the junction of today's Railroad Avenue and Stanley west to Murrieta.

The brick plant was located between the CP and WPRY tracks and was served by both railroads. The plant went through several ownership changes and finally, in 1936, was bought by the Stockton Firebrick Company. Their business increased during World War II. After the war, business declined, and the plant closed in 1949, a victim of the railroad's conversion from steam to diesel. The plant was demolished in 1953.[82]

SP Station Agent W. L. Heaney reported that for the year 1926, the value of exports of minerals and manufactured products greatly exceeded farm and ranch products.[83]

Several doctors working from their home maintained a room they called their clinic. Some even advertised their facility as a hospital. There were no actual hospitals of any sort in Livermore for most of the nineteenth century.

The internationally recognized psychiatrist Dr. John Robertson initially leased and then bought the Livermore Collegiate Institute.[84] He then converted the facility into a pioneering mental hospital. The Livermore Sanitorium became the first hospital in town.[85] The main college building burned in 1931.

Alameda County opened Arroyo Del Valle Tuberculosis Sanatorium along Arroyo Del Valle in the hills south of town. It became well known for its dry climate which eased the patients symptoms.[86] It closed in August 1960, after antibiotics became available as an actual treatment for the disease.[87]

The U.S. Veterans Administration built a hospital on a hill west of Arroyo Del Valle about six years after the end of World War I.[88] The site was also chosen for its dry weather conditions. It expanded to a major facility and is still in service presently.

Dr. Paul Dolan settled and married in Livermore after serving in the army during World War I. Upon his return, he joined the practice of Dr.

James Warner in a private clinic. He continued in the practice after Warner retired. Some years later, Dr. Dolan realized Livermore needed a general hospital. He built St. Paul's Hospital and opened it to all doctors in town in 1927.[89]

Several prominent members of the town were also saloon owners and operators. The board of trustees agreed to increase the number of saloons at a "lively meeting" in 1903.[90] Efforts by local supporters of the Woman's Christian Temperance Union did influence the trustees to adopt an ordinance limiting hours of liquor sales with cold meals between midnight and 5 a.m.[91] The county gave local communities the option of voting to become "dry" or remain "wet." The "Wets" won two to one a Livermore election.[92]

Aviation created much excitement just after the war. Wartime pilots acquired surplus aircraft and went barnstorming to farmers' fields. Pioneer aviator Frank Bryant landed in Luders' field in 1919. He demonstrated stunt flying and sold rides for $10.[94] Other barnstormers visited both Gardella's and Luders' fields. The *Herald* stated, "the first paying airplane passenger on a flight from Oakland landed in Livermore," that same year.[95] Several locals bought airplanes and there was much interest in Federal planning for an airport in Livermore."[96]

Airmail began taking a chunk of the long-distance mail service decades before passenger air travel overtook the railroads. The Commerce Department constructed lighted beacons across the country to aid airmail pilots. This included the beacon on Mount Diablo, visible from Livermore.[97] The beacon has been refurbished and functions for special occasions.

Fuse Works' technical supervisor and his wife, Mr. and Mrs. Grant H. Tod, were killed at the L Street crossing of the WPRY. The trustees had to remind the WPRY of their franchise requirement to maintain the crossings.[98] An irate Mayor William Rees wrote a letter to the WPRY, noting the city franchise required the railroad to install crossing safety devices and limited train speed through town. The trustees also noted that crossing signals should have been installed years ago. The trustees responded that the railroad was in violation of its franchise, which required the railroad to install crossing safety apparatus. The mayor also demanded WPRY reduce freight train speed through town to 10 mph.[99] It was reported that some trains were passing through town as fast as 50 mph. The railroad responded that the speed of the train was up to the engineer, and company officials could not prevent some violations of those orders. Although not stated explicitly, the trustees' letter threatened the revocation of the franchise. The railroad immediately relented and installed signals at the key crossings.[100]

Harkening back to the operations of the USRA, the Livermore Chamber of Commerce asked the State Railroad Commission to authorize an interconnect between the SP and WPRY in Livermore to shorten the route for receipt and shipment of goods. Without it, cars from one railroad with business at a loading dock on the other would have to be transferred at an interchange yard, requiring additional fees and mileage.[101] The request was rejected by the railroads.

The SP, the premier railroad in the Bay Area at the time, was the first choice for all formal services. When President Warren G. Harding died in San Francisco, his SP funeral train crossed the Dumbarton Bridge and then, while passing through Livermore, took on a helper locomotive for the climb over the Altamont.[102]

The Stockmen's Protective Association leaders John McGlinchey and William Wagoner recommended to the SP that new stock corrals be erected at the western end of the yard.[103] WPRY trains started fires that burned more than 1,000 acres at Midway and on the Altamont. Ranchers Michael Mulqueeney and John Flynn sought the help of the association to obtain compensation for their losses from the railroad. A railroad official failed to appear at a meeting of the association to discuss the issue.[104]

The library on Third Street between J and K streets was built with a grant from the Andrew Carnegie Foundation. The Carnegie Library opened May 1911 and continued to be the city's library until 1966. The site, now called Carnegie Park, has changed little since 1911. The park was initially the site of a butcher's slaughterhouse.[105] The Carnegie Building now includes the Heritage Guild office and archives, also a small gallery for local artists.

7

FALLING ON HARD TIMES

The 1929 stock market crash was devastating to Wall Street but initially had little effect on Livermore. The initial local response to the stock market crash was that the financial decline was minor, and recovery was thought to be in sight.

Before the end of the nineteenth century, state laws had considerably altered organization and regulations for incorporated towns. A resolution was introduced to the trustees proposing the town disincorporate and reorganize under the new laws.[1]

The Ordinance Committee investigated the advisability of reorganization. Nothing came of it at that time as the new laws were not being enforced. The proposal was revised seven years later and a bill put on the ballot for a special election. Those supporting reincorporation claimed the original charter limits progress in certain areas. Those opposed were afraid of the dangers and possibilities of higher fees and taxes.[2] The new laws were not yet being enforced and the bill was defeated by a vote of 227 to 59.[3] A revised bill was placed on the ballot four years later, as there was concern the laws would finally be enforced. The bill was passed with 183 votes in favor and 90 opposed.[4]

The board of trustees, still thinking the growth of the Roaring Twenties would continue, felt it was time to upgrade the town to a city. The town's population exceeded 3,000 for the first time in the 1930 census. State regulations after reincorporation only required a petition signed by 25 percent of the voting population for a town to become a city. Maitland Henry, owner and publisher of the *Livermore Herald*, initiated such a petition.[5] The signed petition was presented to the trustees just over one week later.[6] An ordinance was proposed then adopted by the trustees the following month and the town officially became a city on July 29, 1930.[7]

The town's board of trustees became the city council, although there was no immediate change to its makeup. Actual conversion from town to city ways of doing business had been going on slowly for some time and then increased as the population grew more rapidly after World War II.

A year after Livermore was declared a city, jobs were scarce.[8] President Roosevelt's New Deal created the Works Progress Administration (initially the Civic Works Administration), California established the State Emergency Relief Administration, and the city approved a relief bond. The city council initiated projects to create jobs quickly. Initially, street upgrades had been funded by the adjacent property owners. A bond issue to support street paving was passed by six to one.[9] Two years later, the town increased the property tax to support the cost of paving and safety of the streets and roads.[10] Their efforts concentrated on mostly shovel-ready street, road, and highway improvements. Many of the jobs were short term, with employment on a day-to-day labor basis.[11]

Heavy rail traffic through town was reported shortly before the stock market crash. Freight loadings set records in 1928, and the prospects for the following year were even better. The high freight traffic caused the SP to enlarge its office in the Livermore Depot, build a new steel water tank, and lengthen the passing siding.

The railroads faced financial difficulties after the market crash. They maintained high shipping rates and passenger fares, driving off customers and accelerating the development of less expensive ways for local travel and shipping. Rail traffic through Livermore declined and was further reduced by the completion of the Benicia rail bridge in 1930. The Hetch Hetchy project, requiring tunneling through the nearby hills, helped maintain some local passenger and freight traffic into the early 1930s. Passenger rail service diminished during the Depression, becoming useless for local and regional travel before disappearing altogether.

Newspaper articles mentioned significant events but did not necessarily record public leanings. Other sides of several stories were told in oral histories recorded by LHG, including the organization's co-founder Herbert Hagemann's recorded oral history, which is most revealing, providing insider views of the times and is quoted throughout this work.

Herbert Luders Hagemann Jr. was born in 1921 on the Hagemann Ranch and died in 2000. He was a member of the third Hagemann generation owners of the ranch initially owned by Martin Mendenhall. Hagemann often did not distinguish between "ranch" and "farm," likely because they sold farm products, though their main business was raising horses.

He shared his memories of businesses, schools, scandals, alcohol stills, politicians, and other topics. Hagemann recalled the extensive effects of the 1929 stock market crash:

Well, those who had investments—well, everybody had some—they lost. The market crashed. That was the big thing that—I don't think there was ever anybody in Livermore that I knew that went hungry. Cause we lived on the ranch. And if we had hungry friends, we gave them the food. That was the way of the small town, then. Yeah, before 1940 all this was strong. Livermore was healthy. And even with the Depression, Livermore had its captive business here. And the businesses did thrive. Everybody had hardship, but no more than anywhere else. In fact, I think Livermore was a little better off because there were a lot of ranching people around here who did not invest in the stock market and had money. So, there was some capital to put back into the local economy. The major thing was the old Fourth of July parade which, from time immemorial, was a big celebration.[12]

Downtown was still just a few blocks in either direction with the businesses that supported the town. Hagemann noted:

The center of town was from the flagpole, east and west, and this way on the side streets for one block, and that was it. And they went down to L Street. Beyond L Street, it was all warehouses. North, it pretty much stopped at the railroad track, really. And Second Street on the south side. There wasn't very much business on Second Street. The area here was almost strictly agriculture at that time. The big thing were the warehouses. And, of course, in the early days, the warehouse was also a commission merchant. There weren't stores enough in town, why they could get the goods for you and have it shipped in by railroad, and you'd have it. Everything was based on what the rancher did. He sold his crop to the warehouse, and then he went uptown and bought his supply of whatever. And he had, oh, hardware stores, and of course always the grocery stores, and usually carried hardware. And the other businesses, they were all more or less geared to the agricultural system. They were dependent on the agriculture to be their livelihood. The few things that had come in, the Fuse Works, Coast Manufacturing, they called it. The company made explosive fuses. They were shipping internationally and had around two hundred employees before the first world war. Fuse Works had an impact, and they hired quite a few people. Of course, they came earlier. When I was a small boy, they were quite a big thing in the town. There was the Brick Works earlier, of course, very early. And the Brick Works is really very important. It was important to the town, more than it was for the amount of bricks that they exported from here, because people would come from Europe, you know, and the first job they'd take would be at the Brick Works. The Brick Works specialized in fire brick for boilers. Well then in the twenties, Hetch Hetchy began to work here. They were digging the tunnel for the water project for San Francisco. And they hired multitudes of people. I think the town grew a thousand in population while Hetch Hetchy was working. And we saw some temporary new business. I can't remember what they were, but they were here and gone. And the old businesses that were established flourished and continued afterwards. Dropped back to their normal flow of business.[13]

The Hetch Hetchy project built a spur off the WPRY to bring heavy electrical equipment to a warehouse at L Street:[14]

And, of course, the trains. The trains were here. For a long time. But in the twenties and thirties, trains were still a big thing. Trucks hadn't taken over the drayage business yet. We had the Lincoln Highway, but most of the roads hadn't been built. The depot was the center of town. We still had the passenger trains, and if you didn't have a car, you took the train to the city. So, basically, cars were just starting to get into popularity. But they were more of a novelty for transportation. Automobiles were going when I was a kid, you know. My mother saw the changeover; I didn't. I saw the automobiles improve and advance. Most people, if there was something in Livermore they couldn't get—fancy clothes, for instance, or whatever—they'd take a shopping tour in their car. We'd go out on Lincoln Highway and go straight on through Dublin Canyon and on into Oakland. It would sometimes take an hour and a half with the car.

Oh, Livermore had a lot of hotels in the early days. There was the Livermore Hotel by the flagpole, and there was—Well, Mally's sort of ran a hotel right in the middle of the south side of main street. And then down by L there were two. There was the Washington Hotel which was built by Bardellini. And then Mally's bought it later, and they called it the Palace Hotel, and boy some palace. And then across the street was the Valley Hotel. It started out as Germania Hotel. And then there was Hooper's Farmers Hotel. And that became the stage depot.

There was a bakery and a flower shop and a beauty shop, I think, right close to L Street on Main on the north side. That was a hotel, and then it burnt. It burnt many years ago. But the hotels before the automobile, they did a thriving business. They all had little restaurants; you know. Mally's had a fine restaurant at that time. Mally's was the top restaurant for many, many years. In the twenties and thirties. Croce came inhere, and he had a restaurant in the show building, the Schenone Building, upstairs, and he ran a very good restaurant.[15]

The restaurants were all saloons before Prohibition. Mally's and Croce's survived because of their good reputations, although they also secretly sold drinks. Louis Schenone initially grew fruits and vegetables selling them from a peddler's wagon and then opened a store downtown, which was prosperous.[16] He purchased a property on the south side of First Street, between Lizzie and J Streets. There, he built a two-story building with a 500-seat movie theater on the first floor.[17]

Hagemann continued:

> The ladies' shops didn't exactly thrive all the time. But one did, it did, really. There was a lady called Terri MacLean, who had a dress shop, and she became pretty wealthy. But they used to complain. Everybody saw the dress before they bought it, you know. The whole town went to look. And remember, old Mr. Victor had the clothing store. He grabbed me by—in the back of the coat. Fits good. He'd draw it up—They didn't have a tailor, you know. You had to take it as is. But basically, you could get most of the things here. If a few wanted to appear somewhere in a very fancy dress, you didn't buy it in Livermore. So, if you wanted a good-looking thing, you'd go out to San Francisco or Oakland.[18]

There was some turnover of residents by those who did not own property, successful businesses, or regular jobs. A small number of new immigrants usually joined family already present. They lived either with relatives or temporary housing until they could afford one of the few rental properties. Some first took temporary jobs on the farms or ranches before working at the Brickyard:

> Quite a few. Italians, and Germans, and some French. And there were always that nationality of farmers. And they included people—And they, while they were at the Brickyard, they would take citizenship class. Get their papers. And then they would go onto something better, and a good many of them went into business for themselves.[19] There was a blacklist going on before the twenties and into the twenties. I'd say probably up to the time Chamber of Commerce took over. That was a convenience record for the business people. It was a record of those people in town. Let's say you have 2,500 people, and maybe there's fifty of those people, or fifty families, who didn't pay their bills. Like deadbeats, you know. It amounted to—a bad credit rating. Today, you have a credit bureau who handles this stuff for you. So, the Merchants Association—No, not IRS. There are private credit things who investigate a person's credit and give out the information. So, this is what the Merchants Association did in their time. But in a little small town, why they didn't have much to

do. There weren't that many. The association's actions were warnings to the merchants. Watch this guy because he, uh—Get your money, you know. Make him pay cash or something like that. It was a service for the merchants.[20]

An aspect of the frontier days' annual financial management of the ranches continued through the Depression:

I can remember in the kitchen we have the grocery bills on a nail. For the whole year. And at the end of the year add them all up and pay the bill. This was the old agricultural way. Once a year you sold your crop, and when you've sold your crop, say sometime in the fall, everything was done, the cattle were sold, grain crops were sold, you had all your money put together, you went to town and you paid your bill. And then you started again for the next year. Not that you couldn't pay it as you went. This was the custom. That was the way it was geared. But it was the custom. The merchants expected that to happen and the farmer planned on it. And sometimes the farmer thought it was kind of inconvenient, and he'd like to just—There were some who just paid as they did it. In fact, we did. Like in the Depression, that sort of changed a little bit because the farmer would come in with his produce, and he'd trade it for groceries that he needed. So he paid right there instead of having a just cash and carry thing. He just bought it. Paid cash. Or trade. A whole lot of trade. Eggs and butter. See, we didn't have restrictions on dairy products and things that we have today, and we could make butter and sell it. Mother was a member of the Livermore Merchants Association. She was secretary. That was before the Chamber of Commerce was formed in 1926. Very small, but active. Well, the town was small. And as far as bringing in business, futile attempt because there was no need for it. That is, you know, there was no need in the Bay Area to expand out this way. So, they simply took care of their own. And they did bring some things in.[21]

On the eve of Prohibition, the county adopted more stringent saloon laws.[22] The trustees adopted a new saloon ordinance, after which a saloon lost its license for selling beer to a woman.[23, 24] The short-lived *Livermore Journal* supported and announced the Methodist Anti-Saloon League's "dry" sermons, while ignoring "wet" activities of the Churches, and saloon operators.[25]

All Livermore saloon licenses were suspended in response to new county rules during the ratification process of the Eighteenth Amendment to the Constitution.[26] The local saloons converted to ostensibly dry, soft drink, and juice bars or gambling parlors.[27] Nothing was said about what was available in a back room or basement. With Prohibition, most of the saloons were transformed into coffee shops, gambling houses, and a juice bar. Frank Gardella's soft drink parlor, formerly a saloon, had a back room with a 20-foot-deep hole in the floor and rocks at the bottom. So when the feds came in the front door, whiskey bottles could be dropped down the hole destroying any evidence.

Multiple raids, arrests, fines, and imprisonments increased, the editor of the *Herald* noted, "Livermore was face to face with Prohibition enforcement."[28] Gardella's restaurant was a first-class restaurant and café on the second floor of the Schenone building.[29] Brothers and restaurant owners J. P. (Jack) and Frank Gardella, along with three deputy sheriffs, were indicted by a grand jury for graft and conspiracy.[30] The county sheriff and three deputies were forced to resign having been present at Croce's and failing to make arrests at earlier incidents.[31]

Hagemann noted:

There was a big ring of bootleggers up and down the coast, and some of our major people in the county area were a part of it. Earl Warren was one of the big people in it.. Yeah. At the time he was district attorney for the county. Yes, it was incredible. Jack Gardella was the—the front. He sold it. He sold the stuff. It was all illegal. I can remember my dad bought an old Dodge from Ed Aylward, probably a 1916 car. The only thing that worked on the dashboard was the oil gauge. He was going to have some kind of a get together, so he went to Jack Gardella to get some liquor. And what he did, he'd take your car and go get it and bring it back to you and then he'd drive away in his own car. Yeah, then he'd go get it for you wherever the secret place. I don't know where it was. But I can remember he came back, and he says—He was a character. "Why didn't you bring your good car. Suppose I have to make a getaway." There was a big investigation going on, and sometime around like twenty-nine or thirty, they raided the still. And Jack Gardella—They raided the whole thing. The whole organization. It was up for grabs. So, they made a deal. And somebody had to go to the slammer, San Quentin. So, they paid Jack Gardella to do it. He went to San Quentin for—I don't know how many years, two or three or whatever—and when he came out, he got $400 a month, which Depression days was a lot of money. And every 2 years, he got a new LaSalle or new Cadillac. That went on for years and years, and as soon as Earl Warren was made governor, he pardoned Jack Gardella, first thing, so that he could vote and hold public office. And then he became a Supreme Court justice. It was something like the district attorney knew of this Prohibition, but he knew about the alcohol production but was in on it anyway. He was in on it, yeah. So that's what happened. Of course, like the payment, the new car and the so much a month, there's no way to prove it, except I heard it from Jack Gardella's nephew.[32]

Anna Siig, LHG co-founder, confided that her father was proud of his stash and drank more during Prohibition than either before or after. She also noted that some years back, while researching the history of Wente (Vineyards), they did not admit to selling wine out the back door. However, interviewing a long-time former Wente employee, he admitted, "men had to find a way to feed a family." Siig also said that there were tunnels from so-called "dry" establishments to secret liquor stashes.[33]

Wente, Concannon, and Buena Vista wineries continued operating during Prohibition by making and selling sacramental wines. Wente did not have a church contract and partnered with Buena Vista which did. Concannon had a separate church contract. Concannon survived those bleak Prohibition years under very close scrutiny of federal agents who would closely monitor not only the production but also the sales of wine. They had to obtain their approbation each year from the bishop of the diocese that they provided for.[34]

The seniors of the Presbyterian Church recognized that the saloon businesses were a significant factor in the income of many members of the community. They agreed not to inform the authorities about what they might know about it. They also noted there were more ambulances in town than before or afterwards.[35]

Little Mexico was partially demolished when the Lincoln Highway was built on what is now Portola Avenue.[36] The Caratti brothers, Joe and Jack, bought the dance hall. They refurbished the building and named it the Arrow Highway Inn located along the newly established Lincoln Highway north of town. They closed the inn for the duration of World War I and afterwards reopened it as the Over The Top Restaurant.[37] The restaurant later became Joesville Diner.

The properties along the highway west of Livermore Avenue and north of the town line, became known as Joesville. The dancing girls and other "entertainment" continued in Joesville. Camp Comfort was a place of "entertainment" opened for Hetch Hetchy workers. It was located along the road to one of the tunneling sites, adjacent to what is now Sycamore Grove Park, south of the town line.[38]

Dances proliferated through the Depression, replacing the traditional annual balls for most organizations. The availability and cost of live musicians precluded them from becoming a ball. The Lions Club, which was formed in 1924, and the Eagles Club both put on multiple dances

Club Joesville Diner. (*Livermore Heritage Guild*)

throughout the year. The annual Fireman's Ball, which had supported the town band for fifty years, no longer existed. The firemen continued sponsoring dances to celebrate holidays, the rodeo, and support widows and orphans.[39] The local chapter of the American Legion had been hiring the band for its dances and adopted the band financially and took on its management.[40]

Alameda County provided the town funds to construct a building commemorating the World War I veterans and dead. The American Legion bought the property at Fifth and L streets which it donated to the county. The Veterans' Memorial Building, completed in 1931, became a venue for dances, performances, and also served as the headquarters for the local chapter of the Legion.[41]

Livermore resident and boxer Max Baer was sometimes known as Madcap Maxie. The town went wild after he defeated Max Schmeling to become the heavyweight champion of the world in 1934.

Baer's victory created the biggest celebration in the history of the town according to Max's older sister, Frances May. The town band played in front of their house as hundreds of visitors surrounded it for two days. The Eagles put on a parade through town.[42] Max, half Jewish, became a hero of the Jewish population as Schmeling was Hitler's favorite.

The years of Prohibition created a disaster in the wine business as vintners were let go and equipment became obsolete. The end of Prohibition in 1933

Max Baer. (*Public domain*)

began the revitalization of the local wine industry. Small numbers of cases of bottled wine were shipped by express in baggage cars. The small loads were carried in baggage cars on scheduled passenger trains, not with the arbitrary schedules for box cars on freight trains. The shipping costs were based on weight and volume by destination fees rather than carload miles. It was a long, slow struggle after Prohibition for the wine industry to regain its economic position and took decades for the winery business to recover.[43]

Livermore's performing and fine arts associations largely disappeared during the Depression, though the arts continued in school programs. Occasionally, dances had to be canceled because there were no bands or orchestra as musicians were drafted for World War II.[44]

The state had the WPRY through Livermore on a relief project list for potential grade separation at east First Street. In an early hint about the possible consolidation of the trackage of the two railroads, the city council asked for the SP crossing to be included in the project, but the project was never funded.[45]

With increasing automobile and truck traffic, the city requested the railroad remove the crossing warning wigwag from the middle of First Street at Maple and replace it with new, flashing-light signals on each side of the street.[46] The railroad responded that the city was responsible for the cost of moving the signal because the city ordered that the wigwag be placed in the middle of the street nearly twenty years earlier.[47]

The federal government decided to establish an airport in Livermore.[48] The government initially leased and then bought Anton Gardella's field.[49] The Department of Commerce controlled the field reserving it for mail, military and commercial use.[50] The field was enlarged with a 4,000-foot runway.[51] Control of the field was transferred to the navy and remained available for military and commercial aircraft but not for private aviators. Mrs. Eleanor Roosevelt's plane made a stop there and was greeted by many Livermore residents.[52]

A horrendous head-on collision of WPRY's *Exposition Flyer* with a locomotive in transit occurred in 1940 near Pleasanton. The wreck killed three people, injured twenty-one, and destroyed both locomotives. The cause was attributed to an incorrect time setting of the transit engineer's watch. It was never ascertained whether it was truly an accident or sabotage.[53] It was also noted that the WPRY, still in receivership, had never installed block signals. The railroad was still using a train-order system that gave a train clearance to use a segment of track for a specific time. It made no provision for trains that were not aware of being off schedule or were in the wrong place at the wrong time. Automated block signals, used by the SP since 1909, would have prevented the accident.

The Depression became the death knell for SP's Livermore passenger service. Service declined beginning with the cancellation of the early morning mail and newspaper train. That train normally arrived at 3:23 a.m., provided the newspapers for the morning news carriers and mail for the post office before opening time. Arrival on a later train at 9 or 9:30 a.m. was unacceptable to the news dealers and they moved to trucks.[54] The SP removed three passenger trains, reducing service to one train in each direction daily.[55] A few months later, SP claimed they would continue passenger service.[56] The ICC prevented the complete abandonment of services as long there was no parallel service from another carrier. In November 1940, the SP requested that the State Railroad Commission allow the complete removal of service on the line through Livermore.

The railroad claimed the WPRY provided comparable passenger and mail services.[57] Both the commission and the ICC ignored the fact that the WPRY service was not comparable. SP terminated service between Oakland and Sacramento for trains No. 231 and No. 232 via Niles Canyon on January 22, 1941. Those train numbers refer to the two directions of the same train. It was known here in town as the Livermore Local. The train ran from Sacramento to Oakland in the morning and back in the afternoon, providing the last SP scheduled passenger stops in Livermore. The cancellation of those trains ended seventy-two years of CP passenger service in the valley.[58]

The last scheduled SP passenger train in Livermore. (*Elliot Dopking photo, John Sarboraria collection*)

The Lions Club met with the Garden Club to encourage the planting of Victory Gardens shortly after the U.S. entrance into the war.[59] Alton Scott, school district superintendent, announced a Victory Garden would be planted across the street from the elementary school at Fifth and J streets. Each grade from kindergarten to eighth would have a 10 by 10-foot plot. At the same time, the Lions Club announced it would award prizes for the students' products to encourage participation.[60] There was a tremendous response from students throughout the school district including Mocho and May schools. A truck was needed to haul the produce which was given to the sanitarium. A public meeting at the high school was arranged by the chamber of commerce. The high school announced special classes and the water company announced reduced rates for Victory Gardens. The Lions Club also sponsored a competition for the general citizenship. Photographer Elliot Dopking won the competition in 1944.[61] The competitions all concluded with the end of the war.

The U.S. Navy purchased a square mile of farmland from W. Gatzmer Wagoner in the days following the Pearl Harbor attack. The navy immediately started the construction of Naval Air Station Livermore, which was in service by April 1942 and located about 3 miles east of downtown Livermore. The air station had good ground transportation

The Naval Air Station, Livermore. (*Public domain*)

from two railroads and U.S. Highway 50. It served thousands of pilots and aircraft during the war, and navy personnel supported the city's business during the war. They lived on the base and moved on after the war. They did not significantly alter the city's permanent population. The base was closed and declared surplus in 1946.

8

RAILROADS DETERIORATE

Rail service nationally peaked in the 1920s. The economy was still dominated by the railroads in 1929. Freight loadings set records in 1928, and the prospects for the following year were even better. Both local and long-distance passenger traffic were increasing. The railroads hardly appeared to take notice of the impending competition from automobiles and later, airplanes but made incremental improvements to enhance their operations.

The stock market crash took a considerable toll on the stock value of the railroads and forced those in debt out of business. The Depression reduced their freight traffic and profits. Passenger services, which were always operated at a loss, became a greater burden. Paving of roads made local, then regional automotive travel, more convenient.

By the 1930s, automobiles had surpassed the railroads in passenger miles.[1] Local trucking rapidly became more efficient for items such as newspapers, mail, and milk, by not requiring transfer to and from rail and horse-drawn wagons.

The trust-busting era ended government support for rail projects. Public enmity continued to grow. The government spent $1.8 billion on roads but virtually nothing to support railroads before the Depression.

The railroads kept ticket fares, express, and freight prices high, which further encouraged automotive traffic. They lost local passengers through the Depression, reduced local services accordingly, and eventually eliminated them altogether.

The federal government only allowed the elimination of a service when there was a parallel service. SP claimed its passenger service through the Livermore Valley was parallel to that of the WPRY and was eliminated in January 1941.

Long-distance travel was still the province of the railroads. However, they became aware of the potential for competition from passenger aircraft and invested in improving long-distance rail travel. They were experimenting with diesel locomotion which required less maintenance and support than steam. However, they were not able to significantly reduce the number of employees until steam was eliminated after the war.

A pair of SP Livermore station plan drawings chronicles the station infrastructure of both railroads. Although cataloged as 1926–1959, one drawing contains a notation dated December 1961. The drawings were started in 1926 and covered significant changes that defined the station plan into the 1970s. The drawings were revised in 1927, 1930, 1947, 1959, and 1961. They cover the areas west (sheet 1) and east (sheet 2) of L Street, respectively. There is some overlap of the drawings across L Street. The maps contain much detailed information including survey marks, telegraph lines, even the weight of the rails. The drawings are 25 by 56 inches each and are too large to be reproduced in this volume. Drawn with India ink on linen, they were modified as necessary as services changed. The modifications appear to be mostly erasures, done by scraping away the ink. Chlorine bleach was also used to aid erasure. Image enhancement allows most of the erased details to be visible. The erasures appear as lighter or white areas on the enhanced images of the drawings. In some cases, holes in the linen were patched and portions reinforced with additional glued-on linen.

The CP/SP and WPRY are both detailed on the drawings. Infrastructure for both railroads reached its peak in the late 1920s. SP, with forty-one years longer history and owning greater station property, had by far the greatest infrastructure. The larger number of sidings in the SP station represented the number of businesses being serviced. Also apparent is that most of the erasures are on the SP, with almost none on the WPRY. These changes are both indicative of the level of service to the town provided by each of the railroads and the fact that the establishments serviced by the SP were mostly older and many were lost to the Depression. Additional information about the customers' facilities can also be found on the Sanborn fire insurance maps.

The SP house track split from the main track just west of Livermore Avenue and reconnected to the main west of S Street. A crossover just west of L Street allowed the house track to also service the helper locomotive service area. The downtown service siding split from the main at the First Street crossing and connected to the house track between South Q and S streets. It ran nearly 200 feet south of the mainline, closer to First Street. It largely traces the southern boundary of Mendenhall's gift to the railroad. Three sidings split to the north of the passing siding. Two stub sidings ran east from a private road that was to become P Street. The first siding extended from between P and L streets. It ran between the passing siding and Railroad Avenue, ending behind Kamp's furniture store on L Street. The second ran on Railroad Avenue initially to L Street but was eventually cut back to only serve the Livermore Barrel Factory just east of Q Street. A CP stock corral, which had been located on the north side of the tracks opposite the depot for nearly sixty years, was gone, replaced by a corral on a short loop siding near S Street. The station plan also shows a private crossing at what was to become P Street. Stock corrals on both railroads were gone by 1968, closing nearly 100 years of service to one of the valley's earliest businesses.

On the drawings there is no sign or erasure of the old wooden tank north of the CP/SP main, although it still appeared on the 1926 Sanborn fire insurance map. The new and last water tank was demolished after the end of steam in the late 1950s. It was west of L Street, south of the house track. It still appears on one of the drawings but had been erased from the other.

Many of the modifications on the drawings show the remnants of earlier services that had once been present through the center of the CP/SP station property. The remains of the engine house and turntable are gone, although the turnouts are still indicated. The eastern portion of the downtown siding was removed, as well as the western portion of the house track. The service sidings north of the main track were subsequently removed to facilitate the Railroad Avenue project. Erasure of a portion of the depot chronicles the shortening of the freight shed and was probably the last (1961) modification of the drawing. Only two major businesses requiring rail service remained between the original downtown siding and the main track, the Diamond Match Company and Richfield Oil. The Diamond Match Company had a large lumberyard on railroad property which ran from L to N streets and survived into the 1960s. The most significant erasures at the western edge of town were of the Kaiser Paving Company quarry and the Stockton Fire Brick Company plant. The location of the brick plant was between the two railroads with sidings. This duplication is a prime example of unnecessary parallel service provided by competing railroads vying for the same business.

The WPRY's technical advantages did not mitigate their commercial failures, particularly of passenger service. Despite the apparent success of the Inside Gateway, the Western Pacific Railroad Corporation fell into receivership again in 1935. It was operated by the court for nine years through World War II and emerged from receivership without a change of name in 1945.[2] The savior of the reorganized WPRY was the increased long-haul freight demands of the war.

A few experimental diesel-electric locomotives were coming into service. They were initially small, low-powered, and used mostly in yards for switching and for local freight. In February 1930, the SP was testing a diesel on the Altamont grade. It was declared both powerful and fast. The *Livermore Herald* described it as a "new type of electric car with electricity generated by a huge oil powered motor."[3] The locomotives were proving themselves, and within the decade, several companies started to develop and build them.

The Ford Trimotor, the first commercially successful passenger airliner in late 1927, opened the door to well-healed adventurous travelers. It encouraged the founding of several airline companies. Its cruising speed was only just above 100 mph and its range less than 600 miles. With the need to regularly stop for fuel and the vagaries of the weather, it was probably less reliable and often slower than the best passenger trains on the longer runs.

Through the 1930s, airlines were emerging and threatening the high-end, long-distance passenger market. The Douglas DC-3, in service from 1936, was twice as fast and had three times the range of the Ford Trimotor. It was able to cross the country in eighteen hours with only three stops. The airplanes were somewhat cramped for space and had limited onboard services.

The railroads finally responded by developing luxury service with new streamlined trains. They were slower than the airplanes but a lot more comfortable, with excellent onboard services. The new streamliners appeared in the west on the namesake services such as the City of San Francisco, Overland, the Daylight, and the Sunset Limiteds.

With the completion of the WPRY, the Gould family also controlled the Burlington, the Missouri Pacific, and the Denver, Rio Grande & Western, known collectively on Wall Street as the "Gould Roads," and were the first to introduce streamliner service with the *Denver Zephyr* between Chicago and Denver in the early 1930s. This was the initiation of the campaigns by all of the long-haul passenger railroads to compete with the burgeoning airlines. The WPRY and DRG&W jointly agreed with the other Gould Roads to try expanding the service from Chicago to San Francisco. The railroads tested the entire route to demonstrate that a 600-hp diesel was adequate in the mountains. The test train from Chicago was called the *Advance Zephyr*. It passed through the valley, stopping briefly only in Pleasanton on June 20, 1934.

The *Zephyrs* represented a major achievement in passenger train technology. The trains used the first diesel-electric locomotive specifically designed for high-speed operation. With only a 600-hp engine, specially designed, lightweight streamlined cars were developed. The *California Zephyr* was conceived to compete with the Overland Limited.

Advance Zephyr in Pleasanton on June 20, 1934. (*Museum on Main*)

It is this author's contention that the reason the WPRY chose Pleasanton and bypassed Livermore for *Zephyr* service was Hearst's influence and continued animosity towards the SP octopus. Both railroads had stations serving Hacienda del Pozo de Verona, the estate of Hearst's mother near Pleasanton.

The UP and SP jointly acquired Pullman streamlined passenger equipment and started the City of San Francisco service from Chicago to Oakland in 1936. War profits afforded long-distance passenger carriers the opportunity to modernize their equipment and improve service. Competition was fierce, not only from the emerging airlines but from parallel railroads. The flood of new orders for the luxury passenger streamliners overwhelmed the builders.

Depression, receivership, and the war delayed WPRY from ordering its train sets from the Budd Company until October 1945. The *Zephyr* concept evolved to use all diesel power, lightweight stainless-steel cars featuring the newly invented vista-dome cars. Sufficient equipment to commence service was finally delivered almost four years later. Investment in streamliners by both the SP and UP started before the war and increased immediately thereafter. *Zephyr* service finally was inaugurated in 1949.[4] The *Zephyr* ran through Livermore but never stopped. Livermore was dropped from the public timetable for the *Zephyr*. Pleasanton was a flag stop, where the train only stopped to pick up and discharge passengers by prior arrangement, and only for those traveling to or from Salt Lake City and beyond.

Before the war, the railroads saw the diesel (diesel-electric) powered streamliner as the answer to the growing airlines. The few larger diesels built at that time were mostly reserved for first-class passenger service. During that same period, diesel manufacturers were developing higher power engines to be used for freight. During the war, steam still dominated but diesels were making inroads. The military procured many small diesel switching engines for their yards. The example and success of the USRA gave the railroads a model for response to the challenge of World War II, thereby preventing renationalization.

SP steam whistles in town were initially mistaken for an air raid warning after Pearl Harbor.[5] The SP started hiring women for the first time to serve as section hands to replace those drafted and volunteering for the military.[6] Late in the war, the Livermore City Council voted to raise the speed limit through town to 30 mph for troop trains and 20 mph for freight.[7] This was the first increase of allowable speeds since 10 mph was set in 1904, which was an increase from 8 mph set in 1876.

The diesel locomotives could not individually challenge the power of the largest steam locomotives. Sprague's concepts allowing the coupling of multiple electric units together was also applied to diesels. This created the ability to harness almost unlimited power controlled by a single engineer. The advantages of the diesels were quickly recognized by the entire railroad industry. Experience with diesel locomotion was growing and the railroads began making decisions to convert from steam. The last WPRY steam locomotives were built in 1943, and SP's last steam locomotives were built in 1944. Locomotives are expensive, and the railroads had built a large inventory, many still serviceable after fifty years. The unexpected rapid dieselization over the next decade, consequence of the rising cost of labor after the war rapidly sped the conversion from steam. Diesels required less maintenance and needed only one crew for any number of diesel units.

The last steam locomotive in commercial operations passed through Livermore in 1956.[8] All steam locomotives were retired from WPRY service by 1953 and from the SP by 1958. Both railroads retained a few steam locomotives for subsequent railfan excursions, and some were donated for display to cities, parks, and museums. A few were sold to minor roads and the rest cut up for scrap.[9]

Both the SP and the Santa Fe made plays on Wall Street and to the ICC to acquire the WPRY. The attempted acquisitions created considerable interest in Livermore and across the nation. The SP bought 10 percent of WPRY stock in 1960, beginning an effort to quell competition and eliminate parallel trackage. To protect its connections and customers, the Santa Fe then bought 20 percent of WPRY stock. Both railroads petitioned the ICC to allow the buyout of the WPRY.

SP offered a straight one-to-one stock trade. Santa Fe offered one and a quarter of its shares for one share of WPRY. UP backed the SP offer, while GN backed the Santa Fe.[10] Livermore preferred the SP proposal because it would have led to consolidation of the tracks through the city, although it had no say in the matter. The WPRY was then profitable and wanted neither. Eisenhower's Justice Department intervened, contending either merger would violate the Clayton Antitrust Act of 1914.

The last WPRY passenger service that allowed a flag stop in Livermore was a single diesel, self-propelled car built by Budd called the *Zephyrette*. The WPRY kept their steam local service functioning until the start of its *Zephyrette* local in 1950. The *Zephyrette* mostly served as a shuttle for the train crews but was useless for local transportation or connecting with the *Zephyr*. *Zephyrette* service began in March 1950 and ended on October 2, 1960, eliminating the final vestige of mainline passenger service to Livermore.

The SP's streamlined *City of San Francisco* competed with the best service for business travelers, offering speed and fine whisky instead of scenery. The WPRY advertised the *Zephyr* for its dome cars and scenery. However, by 1961, the airlines had sapped most long-distance passengers and service declined to little more than basic transportation.[11] Public opinion sided with the WPRY to preserve the *Zephyr*. The *Zephyr* soldiered on, despite growing losses, until March 22, 1970.

Crossing collisions increased with greater automobile traffic after World War I. Wigwags were replaced by crossbucks over a pair of larger, brighter, flashing red lights and a bell above.[12] The new signals were better in warning traffic of oncoming trains but did nothing to stop those disregarding the signal. Newly developed crossing gates were being considered by the city for the most important streets after World War II. The gates were costly both to install and maintain. The SP required the city to help underwrite the installation cost. The crossing gates also left the railroad vulnerable to legal action if they failed, resulting in an accident.

The Kaiser Paving Company quarry, established in 1923, had rail into the arroyo connecting with the SP.[13] The quarry was directly south of the firebrick plant on the south side of Stanley Boulevard. Several of the lines erased from the station drawing of the Kaiser facility do not connect to the SP. These erased lines were the narrow-gauge tracks used within the quarry. Narrow gauge was preferred for use within quarries because it was lightweight and easy to reposition as the contours of the quarry changed. A segment of 3-foot narrow-gauge track was found along the arroyo and is in LHG's collection.

Both local and through-rail freight traffic picked up during World War II and then declined in the following decade. The declining rail freight traffic and pressure from the City of Livermore prompted the SP to remove much of the depot's freight platform in 1961 and consolidate trackage at the station. The freight house was shortened, reducing the length of the building from 205 feet to 90. The former passing siding and service sidings north of the main track were removed. The house track remained and became used as the passing siding. Some of the property was transferred to the city to be included in the Railroad Avenue project. The WPRY demolished their unused Livermore Depots.[14]

Livermore was growing, and road traffic around and through town was increasing. A downtown development district was created for a bypass street to be constructed along Railroad Avenue, running from S Street on the west side of town to Maple Street on the east. Railroad Avenue was not continuous over the route, with SP owning considerable sections. SP agreed to pay some of the costs for new crossings, track removal, realignment, and property transfer. Strong local opposition from the downtown merchants eventually sidelined the project for several years.

The relevance of the railroads to Livermore continued to diminish, foreshadowing changes to the stations. Larger volume rail shipments moved away from the depot to sidings at specific business locations. Rail freight to the depot was virtually gone. Small shipments, typically less than a carload, moved to trucks. Images show no boxcars being loaded or unloaded at the freight platform and weeds growing from between the rails, indicating significantly reduced traffic.

Transportation technologies advanced for the war effort. Development led to larger and more powerful diesel engines for both trucks and locomotives. The German invention of the jet engine led to major advancement in the airline industry. The Germans also invented the autobahn, which became Eisenhower's inspiration for the Interstate Highway System. These new technologies and others from the war effort markedly decreased rail freight traffic.

The decline of local freight and passenger services had a profound effect on the operations at the Livermore depots of both railroads. Throughout the 1960s, the depots and station agents lost function and responsibility. Passenger ticket sales were gone. Train dispatching and communication were conducted by radio from Oakland. The few industrial bookings were contracted from a central office and the Railway Express Agency was failing. Maintenance of the passenger equipment was neglected, and by mid-decade the "Limited" designation for many first-class trains across the country was dropped.

The last SP stock corral in Livermore was initially built in June 1926 and used for both shipping and receiving cattle and horses. It was located on a short siding west of Q Street. In the Depression, it became part of what was called the hobo jungle. Henry Rowell's horse business was the heaviest user of the corral during World War II. It finally stood unused for a decade and was demolished in 1968.[15]

The SP shortened the freight house and removed the freight shed in response to diminishing business in 1962. The removal of the passing track on the north side of the main track allowed for Railroad Avenue development. The house track became the passing track but was almost never used because of the dearth of business. A short stub was added east of the freight house. The stub was for the caboose which was used for the accommodation of helper locomotive crews.

Consolidation of the tracks of the SP and WPRY through town onto Fourth Street was suggested in 1961 by former mayor John Shirley, head of the Downtown Development Commission. His interest was to provide the extension of Railroad Avenue for a downtown bypass.[16] At the same time, the SP was already thinking of some sort of consolidation of operations with the WPRY. The original proposal was that SP and WPRY share WPRY trackage across Oak Street. Despite meetings with railroad representatives, nothing came of the consolidation proposal at that time.[17] WPRY and SP rejected the proposal because of their incompatible operational procedures.[18]

The discussions did yield an agreement for the SP crossing at P Street, with the proviso that grade separation be included in a future

The depot after it was shortened in 1962. (*California State Railroad Museum*)

consolidation. The WPRY was not as constrained by the possibility of a crossing at P Street and eventually agreed. It was implemented the next year.[19] However, the WPRY noted that P Street would occasionally be blocked for short periods of time, and the city would need to provide electric signals to divert drivers to L Street when P Street was blocked. The agreement also required the crossings at K and N streets be closed.[20]

The WPRY trains in the siding did at times block the crossing for considerable periods. Rules were instituted that required trains standing on the siding for any duration to be split to clear the crossing. This situation created a problem such that the split train on the siding blocked the view of oncoming trains on the mainline. Crossing gates finally solved the problem.[21]

For many years, Southern Pacific was a conglomerate. Under the umbrella of the Southern Pacific Company were several nominally independent corporations. Southern Pacific Transportation (SPT) owned and operated the railroads and other transportation interests. Southern Pacific Development (SPD) owned and developed properties, including federal land grant and unused railroad properties. Other Southern Pacific-held corporations also owned and operated non-railroad transportation, as well as water and mining interests. Southern Pacific Railroad Internal Network Telecommunications (SPRINT) was an attempt by SP to use its long-distance communications lines and microwave systems along thousands of miles of its rights-of-way. Selling long-distance telephone service to private customers ate into AT&T's profits. AT&T sued Sprint but lost in the courts, which cited the need for competition. In 1983, Sprint was sold to GTE for a cash infusion to help the failing SP Corporation.[22] Sprint retained the subsurface rights and eventually laid fiber cable under much of the original WP/CP roadbed. With SPT becoming less profitable, the corporation strove to maximize profits from its non-railroad corporations.

SPT still had a few customers across the valley in the early 1960s. However, it was already considering abandoning the old CP line from Niles to Tracy. The difficult terrain was slow, required extra power to negotiate, and was expensive to maintain. ICC rules at the time made abandonment all but impossible.

The SP station ceased to generate a profit for the railroad and was only considered by the company for its property value. Livermore's historic CP/SP depot was officially closed, and the agency abolished with no public notice on February 5, 1971.[23] SPD planned the entire station property to become a mammoth shopping center. It was to stretch from Livermore Avenue to S Street, and First Street to Railroad Avenue. It was to be built in three segments, starting with a Safeway supermarket and Longs Drug west of P Street. The main feature was to be a department store complex on the blocks between L and P streets. The project was to be financed by an assessment of all properties within the city. For the project, they were to demolish the depot and eliminate or relocate rails through town.

The city council passed a resolution to have staff bring up the issue of consolidation to both railroads.[24] The proposal was again rejected by the railroads for operational and technical reasons. Both railroads had their own ways of dispatching and communicating with trains, which were incompatible. Thus, they were not willing to consolidate using the same track.

After two years of discussions with the WPRY, SPT announced to the Livermore City Council they were finally applying to the Public Utilities Commission for rail relocation.[25] Rail relocation, different from consolidation, proposed that the two railroads share the right-of-way with their own parallel but independent tracks. There was enough room within the 400-foot WPRY right-of-way to accommodate both railroads, although some property acquisition was required.

Part of the proposal included grade separation for both the SP and WPRY tracks at East First Street, Livermore Avenue, and P Street. Not discussed publicly was the issue that railroads were requiring the removal of additional grade crossings in trade for supporting grade separation of a new crossing. This requirement was particularly true for the WPRY, whose tracks crossed most north–south streets in the Northern Addition. Subsequent crossings required for development, all needed to be grade separated.

The discussions did yield an agreement for the WPRY crossing at P Street, with the proviso that grade separation be included in a future relocation. The WPRY was not as constrained by the possibility of a grade crossing at P Street and eventually agreed. It was implemented the following year. However, the WPRY noted that P Street would occasionally be blocked for short periods of time, and the city would need to provide electric signals to divert drivers to L Street when P Street was blocked. The agreement also required the crossings at K and N streets be closed.

Trains in the sidings did at times block crossings for considerable periods of time. Rules were instituted that required trains standing on a siding for any duration to be split to clear a crossing. This situation created a problem such that the split train on the siding blocked the view of oncoming trains on the main line. Crossing gates finally solved the problem.

At the same time, SPD presented the city council with the plans showing the regional shopping center filling the entire station site. Discussion in the press and at the city council was lively, with much public opposition to the development and proposed assessments.[26] The fate of the depot was not mentioned, and it was absent from the plans.

A month after the presentation of the development plans, the SPD again came to the city council requesting a temporary jog of the tracks between P and S streets. The jog was to be temporary until the full relocation could take place and was approved.[27] The request for the jog was specifically stated in such a way that it would allow the SPD immediate approval to develop the shopping center segment west of P Street.

Nationwide rail strikes were called for by the unions in 1967 and 1970 but were limited by federal intervention.[28] The railroads were severely challenged economically by the oppressive and devastating ICC rules not updated in generations. The Penn Central bankruptcy in 1970 was the biggest business failure in the history of this country. It affected almost all freight and passenger traffic from the East Coast to Chicago.[29] The bankruptcy finally woke the government to the rising problem of obsolete and untenable regulation and ushered in an era of reform. However, it took a decade to implement the reforms that eventually turned the industry around.

Congress created the semi-public non-profit National Railroad Passenger Corporation, to operate a national passenger rail service called Amtrak.[30] Amtrak contracted about half former city-to-city services with the commercial railroads over existing lines beginning service in May 1971.[31] It relieved the historic railroad companies of the legal requirement of carrying passengers.

Deregulation under the Railroad Revitalization and Regulatory Reform Act of 1976, together with the Staggers Act of 1980, effectively eliminated most ICC freight regulations.[32] The reforms required universal freight mileage and weight fees. They allowed abandonment of unprofitable services and encouraged consolidation of parallel lines. The changes eventually resulted in a reduction of long-distance freight rates and the reduction of crew sizes.

Despite the rule changes, bankruptcies and mergers continued. SPT and SPD either operated as the separate corporations they technically were or operated in concert when it was most advantageous to the parent corporation. Their offices were located in the same building, and they had a common mailing address at No. 1 Market Street in San Francisco. The distinction was hardly mentioned or understood by most of the city's residents. From discussion captured in the minutes, it is not clear that even the city council members fully understood the distinction. The SPD representative regularly attended meetings of importance to the development, but SPT was generally not represented. Thus, detailed questions concerning actual track plans were answered to favor the development and not necessarily to adhere to SP standards. Over some protest, the city council approved a Railroad Development Assessment

District to partially fund the relocation.[33] The council then sought funding for underpasses for grade separation at the major crossings.[34]

While the rail relocation project was in the final stages of planning, the depot in the middle of the station site was a major impediment to the SPD's shopping center. In February 1973, the city's building inspector issued a demolition permit to SPD for demolition of the depot. SPD then contracted the demolition to the Abdu Allen Demolition Co. of Oakland. A few days later, that contract was purchased from the company by Otto Birk and Del Sullivan for $500. The receipt for the sale is in LHG's collection. Their plan was to tear down the depot and use the lumber for stables and fences at the Four Seasons Riding Academy in Fremont.[35]

Sullivan revealed their plans to his neighbor, Mrs. Dorothy Rosa, and she was given permission to call the newspapers and others. Subsequent publicity compelled the SPT to place a stop order for the demolition. The city council was asked by Chester Fankhauser to help find a use that would historically preserve the depot and to arrange a meeting with SPD personnel.[36] On March 26, 1973, there was a verbal apology and a pledge to the city council from an SPD representative not to destroy the depot for five years.[37] After some vandalism to the depot, the Livermore building inspector was quoted in the newspaper as saying that the building was a fire trap and he wanted it out of his city.[38]

In April 1973, the Livermore Heritage Guild was formed specifically to save and restore the depot. A letter to LHG founding member Janet Newton from a spokesman for SPT, indicated SPT and SPD were cooperating in the station-site development and that the depot must be removed from the property.[39] This letter seemed to indicate the March SPD apology and pledge to the city council, as well as later claims of miscommunication, were disingenuous.

A new demolition permit was issued by the city's building inspector, when preserving the depot was on the agenda for the city council meeting the following Monday.[40] The building inspector's son recently disclosed that his father had been pressured to issue the demolition permit by "higher ups."[41] The council voted for LHG's proposal to preserve the building.[42]

Neither the SPD representative nor the city manager and building inspector were at the meeting. No one informed the demolition contractor or SPT personnel of the council's decision. Actual demolition had begun earlier that day, just hours before the council meeting. *Valley Times* news photographer Lee Estes discovered the ongoing demolition on Wednesday morning. He immediately notified his editor, Barry Schrader, who then alerted both the city manager and LHG members. The latter gathered at the depot and physically interceded until a stop order was processed.

At that point, much of the interior had been stripped and little remained of the building but the exterior shell. A member of the demolition crew remarked that if the bulldozer had started that morning, it would have been all done.[43] Newspaper headlines read, "Communication Breakdown Almost Erases Landmark Depot." Years later, Schrader noted to this author that headline was the city's line and not what actually happened.[44]

Afterwards, several letters with various proposals passed back and forth between the SPD spokesman, the city manager and the LHG. At that time, SPD offered to give the depot to the city but required its removal from railroad property.[45] Since there was never an agreement or plan to move the depot, the offer was dropped. A month later, a spokesman for the SPD recognized the city council's commitment to preserve the depot and apologized to the council for the "mix up" of the second attempt to demolish the building. He stated that SPT, the actual owner of the depot, was a separate company. He also noted they rarely communicated with each other.

Commuter services were always unprofitable. Consequently, the railroads strove to transfer the costs and services to the communities. Some commuter and regional services have trackage rights on existing lines but are not allowed to interfere with the freight. Local consortia with tax support are required to maintain or initiate regional commuter services. Passenger rail development is a long-term process subject to changing political whims and economic forces cooperating across political boundaries of a consortium.

New regional service requires either trackage rights on, acquisition of existing rail or new rail construction. The Class 1 railroads were built when land was available or cheap. Now, UP is the only existing rail through Livermore and the valley. New rail requires the acquisition of a right-of-way, particularly costly in the Livermore Valley. The valley has been highly developed and is now highly valued. Sharing a right-of-way with a major freeway is costly because of the technical challenges. The county acquired the original WP/CP Niles to Tracy right-of-way not connected to the UP, as a corridor for future transportation, after the demise of the SP.

Economic hardships for the railroads continued for decades after the Penn Central bankruptcy and the beginning of extensive changes. SP Corporation failed and UP eventually took over both the WPRY and SP by the 1990s.[46] Just two Class 1 railroads survive today in the West. A Class 1 designation indicates a carrier that earns more than $250 million annually. Union Pacific and BNSF both serve the Bay Area, though only the UP has track through Livermore. BNSF is a consolidation of the Burlington, Great Northern, and Santa Fe Railroads. Their businesses are strictly long-distance freight and profitable.

9

THE CITY AFTER WORLD WAR II

Livermore was declared a city in 1930 when the outlook for development appeared bright and before the impact of the Depression. The relatively stable farm support town, its organization, economy, and population remained essentially unchanged for the next twenty years. Only after World War II did it become a rapidly growing metropolis.

The population, diminished during the Depression, resumed growing slowly after the war. First Street establishments came back to life after earlier cutbacks. The proliferation of automobiles, trucks and increasing development of highways, along with the demise of regional rail passenger service created significant traffic issues, especially through downtown. First Street, in the center of town, became a major state through route.

The most significant development was the extension of the University of California's Radiation Laboratory to Livermore. Radiation Lab director Ernest Lawrence and physicist Louis Alverez, who were exploring sites for their large accelerator experiments, found the unused air station ideal in 1950.[1] The station was a few miles from a population center and had good road access from Berkeley. Functioning existing buildings and room for expansion allowed rapid development. The facility was transferred to the Atomic Energy Commission managed by the University of California, and eventually evolved into the Lawrence Livermore National Laboratory (the Lab), which became the largest employer in Livermore. Increasing employment at the Lab and the adjacent Sandia National Laboratory started a rapid growth of the city's population. The Lab's spin-off companies and the interstate highways continue the rapid population expansion to this day.

Both labs had a profound influence on the demographics and the nature of the city. What had been the support community for local agricultural interests, changed into a support community for the labs, high technology, and eventually the region. The expanding population also spurred the conversion from a rural town to a cosmopolitan city.

Initially, the lab employees and the locals formed separate communities. There was relatively little interaction between the city and the lab located 3 miles to the east, though most employees resided in the city. The lab, a federal government facility, was virtually independent of city management. In later years, the Rotary Club of Livermore, which was founded in 1947, was instrumental in bringing them together.

The Jensen Tract of about fifty homes was the first major subdivision added since the Mcleod and Northern Additions seventy-five years earlier. Located just east of the McLeod Tract, the Jensen Tract was completed at the time the Lab came to the city. The McLeod and Northern Additions along with the Jensen Tract, started filling out in the 1950s. Housing development has continued unabated ever since. Springtown initially a retirement community, was started east of the First Street interchange with Interstate 580 and north of the freeway in the early 1960s. The tract expanded into a major neighborhood for general housing. Properties outside the city limits were incorporated into the city as housing projects were developed.

Local businessmen discussed the possibility of SP resuming passenger service to Oakland. Harold "Hal" Kamp, owner of the furniture store on L Street and a founder of Livermore's Rotary Club, submitted a petition to the SP in 1947. The railroad's response was that there was no possibility of resuming service, as previous patronage was insufficient.[2]

Manufacturers, such as the Brick Plant, the Fuse Works, and the Quarries, ramped up production during the war with delivery mostly by rail. However, these businesses largely declined in the post-war years. The magnesite mine closed because of the high cost of transporting the material from the hills. The Brick Plant closed as the conversion from steam to diesel engines reduced the market for fire brick and the higher cost of magnesite.

The Tesla coal mines closed before the war. Afterwards, former mayor George Tubbs moved forty-five miners' cabins to Livermore, creating a development on an empty block along Railroad Avenue between M and N streets. The cabins were small, rough wooden structures which Tubbs felt were needed for low-cost housing. He called the development Pacific Court, though it later became known as Tubbsville.[3] The block was later called a slum and ghetto.[4] It was eventually acquired by the city and demolished.[5]

The number of Lab employees and their families rapidly became larger than the historic residents and ranchers. The population became much more liberal than before. This created considerable political differences between the two groups. The ranchers wanted unrestricted development to maximize their own profits. The "propeller heads," as lab scientists were called, did not directly profit from development, but were more interested in limited, environmentally sensible growth. The completion of the interstate highways brought in a third political population, commuters.

The tax-supported Livermore Area Recreation and Park District (LARPD) was formed in 1947. Its charter included parks and sports facilities in and around the city. LARPD's first building was constructed at 8th and H streets as a senior center in 1949 and was named to honor its builder, Samuel Bothwell.[6] The Bothwell Center presently continues to be owned by LARPD as a community art and music facility. LARPD as well as the school district are independent corporations not formally part of the city government.

Newspapers espoused the political interests of their publishers and editors. Economically, they largely survived on advertising. The newspapers enlarged as business enterprises subject to speculation, mergers and takeovers by ever larger news groups. They became regional papers making large profits by bringing in higher value advertising while reducing or eliminating most local coverage.

The *Livermore Herald* emerged from the earliest papers in town, remaining the local paper for more than eighty years. The *Echo* remained a local paper for about forty-five years. The owner of the *Hayward Journal* started the *Livermore Journal* in 1919, becoming a short-lived attempt at a regional paper.[7] The *Livermore News* was started in 1947 then merged with the *Herald* and six years later became the *Livermore Herald and News*. The paper was bought by Floyd Sparks, owner of the *Hayward Daily Review* and the *Fremont Argus* which was renamed the *Tri-Valley Herald*, a regional paper, in 1965. Ten years later, Sparks sold his papers to the Media News Group.

The *Pleasanton Times* was bought by Dean Lesher in 1973. He rechristened it the *Valley Times* and moved its office to Livermore.[8] He subsequently merged the paper with his *Contra Costa Times* and the Media News Group creating the *East Bay Times*, which was then sold to the national newspaper chain Knight-Ridder for $365 million.

Graduate school compatriots Joan Kinney Seppala, publisher, and the late David Lowell, associate publisher, founded the *Livermore Independent* in 1963.[9] The paper has a tradition of supporting controlled growth, urban boundaries, and the arts, and is in turn supported by local advertising and donations. The *Independent* is delivered free to residents and is now the only local newspaper in Livermore.

The increasing number of well-educated and multi-talented Lab employees began bringing back cultural activities diminished or lost during the Depression and war. Performing and fine arts had continued in the schools providing occasional public activities through the war, but community-based activities had largely vanished.

The Livermore-Pleasanton Community Concert Association was formed in 1948 to bring in visiting musicians. Their first concerts included New York's Metropolitan Opera contralto Cloe Elmo and nationally celebrated pianist Jorge Bolet.[10, 11] The Livermore Art Association formed in 1957, annually presents both indoor and outdoor exhibits for local artists.[12] They also exhibit at the Bothwell and Carnegie Buildings and library.

New community-based theater, orchestral, and choral groups evolved as the population rose. Livermore High School music teachers started an orchestra and chorus as evening adult education classes in 1953. They invited community musicians to join, including those with little or no experience.[13] Neither persisted more than a few years.

A small drama group called the Cask and Mask Players was formed in 1955.[14] Highly regarded, they performed in the sanctuary of St. Bartholomew's Episcopal Church for five years before moving into the one-room May Schoolhouse. Cask and Mask disbanded shortly before the school was destroyed by arson in 1979.

The local chapter of the American Association of University Women organized the Livermore-Amador Symphony. Both the symphony and the Valley Concert Chorale were started in 1963 and included members of the Labs.[15, 16] They were organized as formal non-profits and continue to the current time. Rehearsal and performance venues were limited to school gyms and rooms, early on. The new sanctuary of First Presbyterian Church became the performance venue for the symphony and the chorus moved into St. Bartholomew's new sanctuaries after they were constructed. The barn built on Pacific Avenue was the National Guard headquarters until 1930. After World War II, the barn became an alternate venue for art exhibits, musical rehearsal and performance, and large Rotary Club meetings. Currently, the barn is now owned by the city but closed for public events because of building code and structural concerns.

The demand for domestic wines surged with the cutoff of European products caused by the start of World War II. The resurgence of local winemaking after Prohibition also spurred the making of barrels. In late 1939, the Canton Barrel and Bag Company of Ohio opened the Livermore Barrel Factory. It was located on the north side of the SP's Railroad Avenue spur in the building of the former Pioneer Winery. The building was between N and O streets, about where the Bank of America office is today. It specialized in making the wooden barrels, with capacities from

12 gallons and upwards, used for aging the wine. Some of the barrels that could hold 6,500 gallons and more were so large they could only be delivered by rail. In their first year, they delivered a 250,000-gallon tank to Cresta Blanca winery and shipped 150,000-gallon tanks by rail to Roma Wine Company in Fresno. Expansion of the operation was limited by the lack of space and skilled coopers.[17] The company eventually moved its West Coast manufacturing to the Santa Rosa area and is still in business. The large wooden tanks were eventually replaced by stainless steel, which were assembled in place and did not require the transportation capabilities of the railroad.

The San Jose-based rose growers, Jackson and Perkins, experimented with growing roses on land leased from the Hagemann Ranch. They discovered that soil, weather, and available water were ideal.[18] They leased the land from W. Gatzmer Wagoner that was to become the now defunct naval air station and grew 750,000 rose bushes a year at the end of the 1930s.[19]

Foreman George DeVor and others started their own rose businesses. Roses became a major cash crop in the valley with 12 million plants grown annually.[20] Jackson and Perkins and others experimented with creating new varieties, some of which won national acclaim, including the Rose Bowl rose.[21, 22] DeVor donated 200 bushes to the landscaping for the new Valley Memorial Hospital.[23]

Alameda County established a tax on rose fields causing several growers to say they would move.[24] The spreading of a bacterial disease damaging the plants along with increased county taxes caused growers to move elsewhere, essentially ending the business in the valley by 1968.[25]

David Lowell, the associate editor of the *Livermore Independent*, grew roses as a hobby and experimented in hybridizing them, creating prize-winning varieties.[26] Alden Lane Nursery has a large selection of roses and features those locally developed. The nursery was started by Jack Williams and Henry Sharp in 1955. Jack's daughter, Jacquie Williams Courtright, now runs the business.

Joe Caratti owned Club Joesville. He was a rock collector and used them to build an arched rock entrance and brick fireplace and walls of the adjacent saloon. They became known as the Rock House Restaurant and Rock House Deli & Saloon. Joe's daughter, Anita Gandolfo, was willed and still owns the rock house buildings and remaining property after Joe's death. The city incrementally acquired much of Joesville's unused property, most recently at the corner of Livermore and Portola avenues, for the Portola Village shopping center.[27]

Livermore was growing, and road traffic around and through town was increasing. A downtown development district was created to fund a bypass street to be constructed along Railroad Avenue, running from S Street on the west side of town to Maple Street on the east. Railroad Avenue was not continuous over the route, with SP owning considerable sections. SP agreed to pay some of the costs for new crossings, track removal, realignment, and property transfer.[28] Strong local opposition from the downtown merchants eventually sidelined the project for several years.[29]

Good-quality gravel was exhausted from Kaiser Paving Company's quarry in the mid-1950s, and new quarry proposals were emerging. The quarries extracted materials for road work. Some of the proposals were for quarry sites east of Isabel Avenue along the creek south of downtown, also between Livermore and Pleasanton. The local press and city council were adamantly against any site east of Isabel and convinced the county not to approve those sites. Government-supported roadwork during the Depression and war decreased after World War II. Most quarries closed though two still exist between Livermore and Pleasanton.

Into the 1950s, the Tri-Valley region, which comprises the Amador, San Ramon, and Livermore valleys, was made up of relatively small towns surrounded by farmland and ranches. St. Paul's Hospital with eighteen beds had been the only hospital in the region since the 1920s. Inadequate for the growing population, St. Paul's was not equipped to provide critical or emergency care or treat complex illnesses. Plans were developed and fundraising for a new hospital began. St. Paul's served the community until Valley Memorial Hospital opened in 1961. St. Paul's then became Quail Garden assisted living facility.

After Kaiser Paving Company closed its quarry, their property was donated to the hospital project. Valley Memorial Hospital on Stanley Boulevard west of S Street with forty-six beds in two stories opened in 1961. A third story was added in 1969, which increased the capacity to 110 beds.[30] Local leaders also applied for government grants to match the community raised funds. Diagnostic and treatment facilities were added. Eventually Valley Memorial became Valley Care with a second, 167-bed, facility constructed in Pleasanton.

After the war, the Fuse Works switched its development efforts to fiberglass materials and structures. The company no longer required the massive shipments of materials or product and, as a result, it abandoned the use of its rail siding. The company merged with Hexcel Corporation, converting the plant to specialize in composite structures. The plant was eventually closed, and the property developed for housing.[31]

Peter Lum came to Livermore to work at the Lab. He worked at Mally's Grill while waiting for his security clearance then bought it in 1954.[32] Lum moved the business to the north side of First Street. He committed to retain the name Mally's Restaurant and kept it open twenty-four hours a day. Local police would bring destitute people to Mally's where they were provided a meal at no charge.[33] The First Presbyterian Church and the Rotary Club offered to pay for the free meals Lum was providing, however, he never sent an invoice.[34] The restaurant closed in 1996.

The old Livermore Airport located north of Laddsville, had also been controlled and operated by the navy, in addition to the Naval Air Station. Through the next decade, the airport became inadequate for newer aircraft. A new facility was planned for a site 2 miles west of the city.[35] The airport opened in 1965.

Street traffic increased rapidly after the war. The editor of the *Herald* noted in the month after the end of the war from a traffic standpoint, "Livermore's outstanding need is a truck route by-passing the business district. And most unfortunately, no such route can be laid out."[36] At the time, County Road 108 was Vallecitos Road from Niles Canyon Road in Sunol over winding and narrow Vallecitos Pass (Pigeon Pass), becoming Homes when crossing the Livermore city line. It then became First Street through downtown to U.S. Highway 50.

Two plans emerged including extending Railroad Avenue to bypass First Street through downtown and rerouting Vallecitos Road to Highway 50 via Isabel Avenue. The council preferred the Isabel Avenue route.[37] Both plans were eventually adopted but took decades to implement.

A downtown tax district was created in 1961, for developing a downtown bypass to be constructed along Railroad Avenue, running from S Street on the west side of town to Maple Street on the east. Railroad Avenue was not continuous over the route, with SP owning considerable sections. SP agreed to pay some of the costs for new crossings, track removal, realignment, and property transfer.[38] Strong local opposition from the downtown merchants eventually sidelined the project for several years.[39]

Mayor Gardella presented a draft plan to the city council, of how streets and roads should change to accommodate the growth. The plan called for Route 108 to be moved to a downtown bypass. The proposed plan was discussed with the state senator and county surveyor.[40] A study by the State Highway Commission, proposed rerouting the highway, bypassing Livermore either east or west of the city. The council preferred the western bypass.[41]

The city did not have a general plan at the time. The council asked for a plan for population growth to 35,000. The mayor and a planning consultant met with state officials to discuss rerouting trucks one block north of First Street, down Railroad Avenue.[42]

Railroad Avenue existed from its junction with East First Street at Maple to L Street. For the proposal to be viable, Railroad Avenue would need to be extended over SP property to the termination of Holmes Street. The proposal was submitted to the Alameda County Highway Advisory Committee. It was an item in the county's recommendations to the State Highway Commission for inclusion in its 1958–1959 construction budget.[43] No funds were authorized at the time.

The city council adopted its first general plan including the recommendation to build small shopping centers with parking. The plan proposed to move some businesses from downtown to somewhat alleviate automobile and parking congestion.[44] The planning consultant suggested that Vallecitos Road be revised to connect with Isabel Avenue and be expanded to a freeway. The Railroad Avenue proposal was again submitted to the state along with the Isabel Avenue proposal for fiscal year 1959–60.[45] The council received a communication from the state that the Railroad Avenue proposal was filed without further action, in view of the proposal for a future Isabel route as a freeway.[46]

Later, the State Division of Highways defined State Route 84. It was to extend from State Route 1 on the San Mateo coast to Highway 50 in Livermore, initially via First Street. The portion from Sunol to Route 50 included County Route 108 and was defined as a future freeway.[47]

A consortium of developers proposed building a toll turnpike to include Highway 84.[48] The state approved the toll road concept without authorizing funding despite the opposition of the city council.[49] The consortium, needing public funding, looked toward the state and county measures. The state senate voted to ban using public funds for a private tollway effectively killing the project.[50] However, the consortium unsuccessfully tried continuing to raise funds for the next three years.

President Dwight Eisenhower, recalling his Lincoln Highway Convoy and his World War II experience with the German Autobahn, advocated national highways for defense. The Federal Highway Act of 1956 created the Interstate Highway System and the trust fund to help underwrite it.[51] Interstate Highway 580 (I-580) parallels the rail route following Highway 50 from the Bay Area to the junction with I-5 in Tracy. I-680 runs from San Jose through the west valley to Walnut Creek and across the Sacramento River to a junction with I-80 in Cordelia. In San Jose, I-680 connects with I-280 forming a continuous route around the South Bay through Silicon Valley.

City councilmen were concerned that the proposed interchange at North Livermore Avenue would cause additional traffic handling problems. They requested an additional interchange be constructed at Portola Avenue.[52] Councilman Manuel Medeiros expressed a concern that many large, noisy, trucks would use Route 84 through the city from I-580 to I-680. The council asked the state to remove the signs routing traffic through the city on Route 84.[53] The council discussed an ordinance to limit the weight of trucks passing through the city. A report from the city attorney noted council plans would not be effective regarding the state highway.[54]

The council requested state funding for Railroad Avenue assuming SP relocation.[55] The county also requested the state support a Highway 84 freeway from I-680 in Sunol to I-580 in Livermore. The city manager subsequently reported that the State Division of Highways had approved a proposed cooperative project for relocating existing Route 84.

The federally underwritten highway system created commuter accessibility to Silicon Valley and other Bay Area communities. The Interstates became a major force for commuters to increase Livermore's population and increase heavier long-distance trucking. The housing boom, created by the closer ties with the growing Silicon Valley, has been largely responsible for the increasing population. Space for housing and costs in the growing Silicon Valley drove many employees to live in Livermore and beyond into the Central Valley. Housing development happens on a far shorter timeframe than transit development resulting in significant traffic increases.

The McLeod and Northern Additions along with the Jensen Tract, started filling out in the 1950s. Housing development has continued unabated ever since. Springtown, initially a retirement community, was started east of the First Street interchange and north of I-580 in the early 1960s. It expanded into a major neighborhood for general housing.

The city budgets were frugal before the war and continue to be conservative. Developers were required to underwrite infrastructure for their construction as growth accelerated. Building procedures became closely monitored by the building department and inspectors for both the codes and city requirements.

There were only three churches in the city before the war. Multiple churches were established, and the original churches expanded as the population grew after the war. The diverse religions and their facilities included most sects that were not previously represented in the city.

A dance studio was opened by the newly married Carol Jean Famariss and became a staple for youngsters through the next seventy years.[56] Students of the Carol Jean Dance Studio annually participated in the rodeo parade. They raised funds for the hospital and also won medals for acrobatics.[57,58]

Granada High School, the second in the district, started its first class of freshmen in 1963.[59] Chabot Junior College was founded that same year, to serve residents of suburban Alameda County. It established its first campus in Hayward and within a few months was providing three classes a week at Livermore High School and the Lab.[60,61] Chabot then opened a campus in Livermore, a decade later.[62] The Livermore campus eventually was renamed Las Positas College.

After rescuing the depot from demolition, LHG expressed the goal of restoring it and creating a museum using donations and volunteer labor. Their goal was initially thwarted by the SPD spokesman. He claimed they would not allow construction adjacent to active track, even though the process to relocate the tracks was already in progress.[63] However, because of the considerable demolition that had already occurred, restoration would have been an economic challenge for a volunteer organization.

A small fire on the floor in the center of the depot was rapidly extinguished, causing little damage to the structure, although one fireman was injured. The fire, which started from material torn from the interior wall combined with trash, was declared suspicious. A subsequent arson investigation was inconclusive.[64]

Official ownership of the station property was formally transferred from SPT to the SPD just days after the purported arson attempt and two days before the start of construction of the rail relocation project.[65] There was ample indication that SPD and SPT were collaborating, playing "good boy, bad boy" throughout this process.

SPD continued to own the station site, leasing the depot to various companies for the next two decades. The SPD continued to oppose any historic restoration of the depot throughout its ownership, which continued until the demise of SP. Liaho West Corp arranged a lease of the depot with the plan of creating a railroad-themed restaurant, SPD did allow Liaho West its first lessor, to construct nonhistorical additions to the depot directly alongside the track still active at that time.[66]

The twenty-year lease was subsequently assigned to Great American Restaurants, Inc.[67] Nothing in the lease or the assignment required historic restoration of the depot. Liaho West refurbished the depot, making significant nonhistorical changes and further damaging its historic fabric. The company constructed a concrete block kitchen on the outside of the building, directly alongside the track. The east chimney, which had served the upper story, was removed and the west chimney, which had served the waiting room, was reconstructed to mimic the original 1892 chimney. The building was repainted in a color scheme that did not resemble either the original CP or the later SP schemes. The interior, which had been previously demolished, was reconfigured to serve the restaurant. Railroad artifacts not originating from this depot were brought in to enhance the décor. The upstairs was reconfigured to serve as a bar, and an exterior stairway was added as a second entrance to the bar.

The Old Livermore Railway Company Restaurant opened on November 22, 1974, and failed in early 1978.[68] Reasons for its failure were reputed to be poor service and interference from the adjacent strip-mall construction project by SPD. The strip mall was anchored by a Lucky Supermarket, Longs Drug, and the Railroad Café.

The depot sat vacant for about two years after the failure of the restaurant and the expiration of the Liaho West lease. Valley Realty then leased the building and established their practice there commencing August 1980.[69] The business was subsequently bought by Coldwell Banker. In order to complement its real estate services, Coldwell Banker leased offices within the depot to Transamerica Title Co. and architect Michael Farrell, through 1987. Coldwell Banker repainted the building, also in nonhistorical colors: off-white with blue trim.[70] The ten-year 1980 Valley Realty lease was assigned to the family trust of Henry Cupples and Marjorie Martin in 1982, but not recorded or formally cleared until 2007.[71] Further interior changes were made to the depot during the 1980s.

On December 22, 1983, the station property was purchased from SPD by the San Francisco firm Aquatic Park, Inc., Bley, *et al.*[72] The purchase was consummated just two days before the merger of the failing Southern Pacific Company (holder of SPT and SPD among others) with Santa Fe Industries was approved.[73] A series of additional transactions limited the ownership of the station property to Stephen and Sandra Bley, and James and Robert Bisio.[74] The lease of the depot was continued through the property sale. James Bisio subsequently sold his share of the property to the Bleys for $300,000 on June 30, 1989.[75]

10

MODERN TIMES

Livermore, with a current population around 90,000, is now part of the much larger and diverse Bay Area. Former Livermore mayor John Shirley pointed out to this author that the number of jobs in the city should be comparable to the number of households. His statement was very true when the town stood alone east of the Bay Area. Shirley's concept has become less meaningful when two bread winners are needed more often, and many are commuting to other parts of the Bay Area.

The number of jobs per household is increasing because of greater costs of living without commensurate raises in salaries. The economy is altering locations, rates of development of jobs and housing, as well as transportation throughout the region. More commuters meant greater traffic congestion, especially through downtown Livermore. Major town events and activities were dominated by adults. Some after-school classes, a few jobs, going to the movies, and cruising downtown were significant activities for teenagers. Neither homework, sports, nor music lessons consumed all the students' time.

The Rodeo Dance and Parade dominated major town events. Teens cruising downtown was the only significant activity for students after school. Livermore allowed cruising after most other communities made it illegal. Cruisers from outside the city were so numerous as to completely close the downtown. They also uncontrollably increased rowdyism and local vandalizing. The Rodeo Dance also increased downtown rowdyism. Locals were advised to stay out of downtown during such activities.[1] The Rodeo Dance was canceled and cruising was made illegal.[2]

Don Baird is a son of Bobby Baird, a teen in 1974 and a direct descendent of Robert Livermore. On a Saturday night, he climbed to the roof of an adjacent building holding the flag rope of the Mill Square flagpole. He jumped from the building, hanging onto the rope, and circled the pole several times about 20 feet up. With lit road flares fastened to his shoes, it was a spectacular sight seen from large parts of town.

The wood flagpole, standing in Mill Square for ninety-nine years, was cracking at the base. It was too close to the street and had been hit by cars on multiple occasions. It was taken down and a new fiberglass pole erected a bit further from the street in 2005. The old pole was cut into four segments when being removed. The upper two segments were reattached, and the shortened pole was raised in Carnegie Park.

Bay Area Rapid Transit (BART) tax district was started in 1957 with the promise of regional commuter service, with plans including Livermore. BART was formed before the emergence of Silicon Valley and was politically dominated by its founding partners to be a feeder into San Francisco. Other counties in the Bay Area were invited to join BART but declined. Initial service started in 1972 and reached Pleasanton in 1997. BART used new rail and planned to share the Interstate 580 corridor to Livermore. In 2018, BART dropped plans for the Livermore extension with the prospect of serving a much larger population base in the Silicon Valley. Plans for the extension to Livermore were being drawn up at the time of BART's decision.

Recent and long-planned improvements to the local highways have only added to the attractiveness of Livermore and Central Valley housing, thereby increasing traffic congestion. Livermore is still considered over the hill by Bay Area regional planners. It is at a distant edge of the San Francisco-based Metropolitan Transportation Commission's district. Thus, Livermore has received only limited financial support for transit developments through the commission. Partnerships with Central Valley communities and possible large commercial establishments appear to be the most successful avenue for both financial and political support for passenger rail development.

Rising housing costs in Livermore are driving lower-cost development in the Central Valley, attracting lower-wage workers who do not have options but to commute. Housing development happens on a far shorter timeframe than transit development, thus primarily increasing traffic congestion. Central Valley commuters significantly increased congestion on I-580 over the Altamont Pass and highway 84 through Livermore.

Politicians and builders in Stockton recognized the potential for development in the Central Valley if rapid transit to Livermore and Silicon Valley could be provided. They formed Altamont Corridor Express (ACE) and began commuter rail service from Stockton to Silicon Valley in 1998. ACE, with stops in Lathrop, Tracy, Livermore (Vasco Road and Downtown), Pleasanton, Fremont, Santa Clara, and San Jose, is more convenient, reliable, faster, and cheaper than rush-hour automobile commuting. Trackage rights on the UP line through Livermore allowed ACE to be quickly implemented. ACE has been highly successful, and its backers wish to increase trackage rights to expand service.[3] The UP predicts increased shipment from the ports will result in a significant increase in through freights on the line. Thus ACE track rights are not likely to be increased.

Valley Link is a recently proposed new rail development that would connect several towns in the Central Valley to Livermore and BART in Pleasanton. It is being sponsored by a new consortium called the Tri-Valley-San Joaquin Valley Regional Rail Authority headquartered in Livermore. BART has committed to earmark the tax funds collected for the canceled Livermore extension, for Valley Link. The project has raised additional funds and appears to be gaining momentum. Valley Link proposes to use the old, county-owned, CP/SP right-of-way across the Altamont. The old right-of-way is mostly intact, significantly reducing anticipated costs from the Central Valley into Livermore. A new right-of-way would be constructed from Livermore to Dublin BART along I-580.[4] The original Livermore Pass (Altamont) Summit tunnel passes under I-580 and is in rather good shape. The tunnel was lined and repaired in 1909 and has not seen rails since 1986. The sharp curves, steep grades, and limited tunnel height of the old line would not be a problem for modern, self-propelled light-rail passenger equipment.

Spin-off companies from the National Laboratories and an influx of companies from outside have increased local employment, especially in technical areas. Gillig, the second largest transit bus manufacturer in North America moved its factory here, because it is centrally located for the housing of its employees. The new Livermore Outlet Mall, which changed its name to the San Francisco Outlet Mall, now brings in large numbers of tourists. These new companies have increased local employment and population. The new businesses have also significantly increased the city's tax base.

The population of Livermore was nearly constant at about 3,000 from only a few years after its founding until 1950. The housing boom created by the Lab, the interstate freeways and more recently the new businesses, have been largely responsible for the increased population.

When the population exceeded 4,000 and was growing fast, city hall became insufficient for the city's needs. Livermore is a general law city under state rules. That implied there were no requirements to pay council members, the mayor, or administration members. The city eventually needed full-time employees, which required a growing number of hired administrators and staff. Office facilities for the employees outgrew the

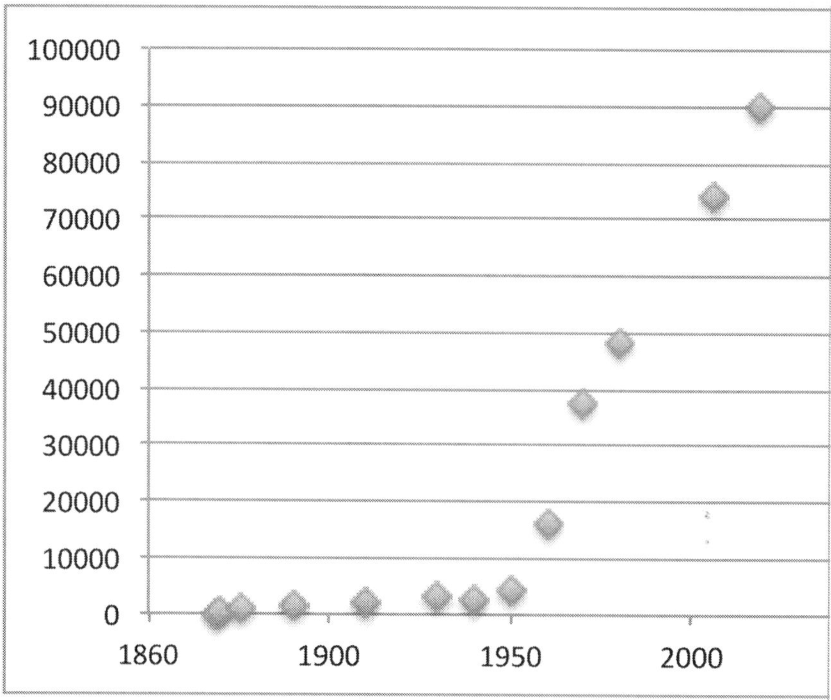

Table of Livermore's population from census data. The population was almost constant from about 1880 growing only slightly in the 1940s. It rose rapidly after 1950 and continued to 2020. Since then, it has been level or eroding slightly. However, new housing development will likely create a rise by the next census. (*Livermore Heritage Guild*)

old council facilities. The city purchased the Bank of America Building on the corner of First Street and Livermore Avenue. The city also acquired other facilities on and around Mill Square to house the newly created and expanding departments by 1957.

The Carnegie building became too small for the growing library. The city started development of a new library and civic center on South Livermore Avenue in 1979. A police building was also built south of the library. City administration moved into an added second story above the Police Building opening in 1979.[5] A temporary city council meeting hall was established in a several-trailer structure on Pacific Avenue, east of the Barn.

Reunions of Old Company I members were celebrated annually until May 1981. Ten former members were thought to have been alive at the time. The few who attended included Clarence and Harold Anderson, Jack Jensen and Robert Livermore, the great-grandson of his namesake.[6]

Three tax districts, the school board, the city, and the Livermore Area Recreation and Park District (LARPD), were all organized at different times with different boundaries. They worked independently for the most part. Schools built in the 1950s and 1960s required significant overhaul by the 1990s. The city's library on South Livermore Avenue was too small, earthquake unsafe, and needed replacement or rebuilding. Support for the Robert Livermore senior and community center on East Avenue was needed by LARPD. Bond issues for each of the above projects had all lost individual elections for capital funding. The executive directors of the three districts proposed a joint capital bond issue that would fund their collective projects. The state required that school bonds must be for the benefit of children. The trustees of the districts convinced the state that all three proposed projects would benefit children. Livermore Public Library and Robert Livermore Center were featured in publicity for the bond although together they were less than one-quarter of the total bond. With strong support from the newspapers, it was passed by the voters.[7] The success of the bond issue established a continuing working relationship between the executive directors of the districts.

The new library building and administration buildings were the second phase of the civic center development. The old library was retained for several years with thoughts of upgrading and converting it to the council meeting chamber. It was earthquake unsafe, and the cost of remediation would have been extreme. The site was cleared for the construction of a new structure for the council meeting rooms and emergency center. The civic center was completed thirty-five years after it began, with the dedication of the city council meeting halls on the site of the old library.[8] The city council chamber was dedicated to Dr. John Shirley, the city's first veterinarian, a highly decorated World War II veteran past president of the Rotary Club of Livermore and former mayor, with a ceremony in July 2019.

SP held on to the station property until it could no longer keep anything. It was sold to the Bley Group of investors just two days before the merger of the failing Southern Pacific Company with Santa Fe Industries.[9] The investors eventually sold the railroad property to developer Anderson Pacific, LLC, of Los Angeles with plans for a housing project incorporated as Livermore Village One LLC in 2005. For the purchase, Livermore Village One secured a loan of $8 million from the city's affordable housing funds.[10] The city council approved the plans which required the move of the depot.[11] The Livermore Village project commenced by demolishing the SPD strip mall, then known as the Lucky Center.

With pressure from LHG, the city of Livermore purchased the historic depot building from the developer for $825,000 in 2007.[12] The purchase separated the ownership of the station property and the depot structure. The purchase again prevented the demolition of the depot but required it be removed from the developer's property. It was argued by this author that moving the depot to the ACE station and refurbishing and returning it to service would be the only way to preserve it in the long run.

The recession, starting in 2008, caused the failure of the development project and the foreclosure of the loan from the city. The station property was consequently deeded to the city and then subsequently transferred to the city's redevelopment agency which continued to manage rental of the building.[13, 14] The final paying tenant was Livermore Downtown Incorporated. Between paying tenants, the depot became an unofficial crash pad for the homeless and was deteriorating rapidly, requiring significant maintenance

The City of Livermore received a grant from the Metropolitan Transportation Commission (MTC) to move the depot to the ACE station and its refurbishment. Scott Hagerty, county supervisor and MTC member, was largely responsible for the grant award. This grant was from the historic component of the Federal Transportation Improvement Program administered locally by the MTC. Of the many terms of the grant agreement, the most important was that it must be used for a "transportation related purpose." Full historic restoration would have been too expensive because of the many changes when nearly demolished and later rented. Some internal updates were required to allow modern service for passengers. The building was returned to service as the ACE railroad and bus depot on August 27, 2018.

Photojournalist Bill Owens published a book of everyday suburban life in Livermore. It was entirely of ordinary people and households, called *Suburbia*.[15] The book was an influential exposé of the middle class in the 1970s. *Suburbia* was included in Andrew Roth's *The Book of 101 Books: Seminal Photographic Books of the Twentieth Century*.

Activist Adam "Fortunate Eagle" Nordwall was a part-native descendent. He was apparently chartered to create a totem pole for the proposed Portola Village shopping center. He dedicated the pole to the indigenous people of the valley. The developer rejected the pole and refused to pay Nordwall when it was completed. He consequently gave the pole to the city to be part of the centennial celebration of the town's incorporation. The city erected the pole in Centennial Park in 1976. However, the base of the pole was in poor shape, so it was buried 4 feet into the ground. Nordwall protested, believing that the 4 feet had been cut off the pole. He publicly cursed the city's sewer system for apparently damaging his work. The sewer system actually backed up a few days later. The cause of the backup was not announced, but the newspapers blamed the curse. Eventually the pole was lifted out, and a steel rod was inserted to support the base. The pole was replaced at full height with a concrete base. Finally, the pole was removed in 2018, as there was massive decay of the wood. The pole was not replaced because it became unsafe. Historians noted that the design of the poll had almost no reference to the native population. Furthermore, the indigenous tribes in the valley never had totem poles.

The city assembled a time capsule to commemorate the centennial of its incorporation. The city manager decided that the capsule should be buried secretly in Centennial Park. No record of its exact location in Centennial Park was to be recorded to prevent its being looted. Many initial attempts with metal detectors were not able to find it. The time capsule was eventually found under the totem pole. The container had deteriorated. Sandia Laboratory provided a replacement, and the capsule was reburied.

An Edison light bulb made by the now defunct Shelby (Ohio) Electric Company, first lit in 1901 at the fire station at First and McLeod, has been glowing almost continuously ever since. The bulb draws 4 watts with a heavy filament. The fire station was replaced by Fire Station No. 6 on East Avenue, and the bulb was moved to the new fire station with full firetruck escort. The bulb was deprived of electricity for only twenty-two minutes during the transfer. *Ripley's Believe It or Not!* stated that the short delay would not mar the bulb's continuous-burning record. The bulb has been continuously illuminated since that move. In 2001, the bulb's 100th birthday was celebrated with a community barbecue and live music. It became news on National Public Radio and was recognized by President George W. Bush.[16]

Michael Madden, the son of football legend John Madden, along with Philip Wente of Wente Vineyards and Joan Seppala, were the primary supporters of Livermore's downtown redevelopment. Madden pointed out that a recent survey in Pleasanton found that nine out of ten business leaders were happy with their location, finding Pleasanton an excellent or good place to do business. They rated Pleasanton's infrastructure and services as good, with the sole exception of entertainment options. In this regard, it appears the bustling nightlife along First Street in Livermore is fast becoming the Tri-Valley's favorite. Madden also noted that the private sector has invested tens of millions of dollars in downtown shops and restaurants.

Livermore High School auditorium was the primary performance venue for musical and theatrical events though inadequate and limited by school functions. Veterans' Memorial Building and local churches were also inadequate. A proposal for a regional theater failed as it was not supported by Pleasanton or Dublin. *Livermore Independent* owner and publisher, Joan Kinney Seppala, a strong proponent of the arts, formed a committee proposing a two-theater project for Livermore. It was to include a small black box theater with about 200 seats and a major performance venue of about 800 seats. Donations supported the planning but no major financial support from the city was evident. The formation of Livermore Valley Opera demonstrated the inadequacy of local venues. This author, a founder and president of the opera company, was invited to join the committee of other performing group leaders to plan a theater in Livermore.

The initial plans were to be non-profit; however, commercial investors required a profit. The Livermore Valley Performing Arts Center (LVPAC) was formed to attract major investors. LVPAC dismissed the original committee and formed a corporation board of regional deep-pocket investors. Consultants' studies indicated a larger theater with more than 1,000 seats was necessary for investment profitability. The plan evolved to build an operationally profitable 500-seat theater as a demonstration to interest commercial banks and investors in a profitable larger theater. The fully functional 500-seat Bankhead Theater was constructed and funded with a combination of community donations and a bank loan. The theater immediately became the primary venue for the Livermore Symphony and Livermore Valley Opera.

Valley Dance Theater was started by Betsy Hausberg in Castro Valley during 1972. She subsequently moved the company to Pleasanton and then to Livermore in 2000. They rehearsed in the railroad depot for a while and performed in the high school auditorium. They now make two presentations a year at the Bankhead Theater including *The Nutcracker* annually before Christmas.[17]

The theater supports resident community companies and also attracts highly profitable traveling performances. The resident companies include the Livermore-Amador Symphony, Livermore Valley Opera, Del Valle Fine Arts, Pacific Chamber Orchestra, Valley Dance Theater, Tri-Valley Theater Company, and the Rae Dorough Speaker Series. The Quest Science Center also hosts free science lectures for students. With the success of the Bankhead Theater, LVPAC's goals evolved for the larger theater to become a regional theater with 2,000 seats.

Further studies indicated that a 2,000-seat regional theater would be profitable, attracting audiences from the eastern parts of the county and even beyond the Altamont for traveling Broadway shows. It was likely the resident companies would rarely use or benefit from the big theater. The original Livermore Village One LLC loan from the Livermore Housing Authority committed the portion of the train station site be used for housing including lower-cost apartments for low-wage workers in the city.

It was negotiated that the required housing could be multi-story, allowing a portion of the property to be free for the regional theater.

Plans for the regional theater coincided with the city's acquisition of the former station property by the redevelopment agency from Livermore Village One. The theater and the city's redevelopment agency agreed to support the LVPAC regional theater proposal to be constructed on a portion of the station site. The remainder of the station site was required to have housing under the terms of the earlier agreement with the housing authority. State-chartered redevelopment agencies were eliminated as the state's economic situation decayed late in the recession. Redevelopment agency funds were continued for projects underway. The theater unsuccessfully tried to continue the big theater development suing the state claiming the theater project was under way.[18]

All LVPAC's income had been invested into construction plans for the big theater, though neither contracting or construction had begun. They risked bankruptcy with the loss of redevelopment agency support. Bankruptcy would have placed both the Bankhead and Bothwell in jeopardy. The resident companies formed an organization, Save the Bankhead and Bothwell. This author's note at the time read:

> The Bankhead Theater is operationally as successful as any community theater in the country and is a testament to the determination and dedication of LVPAC's leaders. The only real solution is for LVPAC, the Bank, probably the City of Livermore and the County of Alameda to come to some mutual agreement to restructure the debt. The bottom line is: if no agreement and soon, no theater.[19]

Banker Cathy Streeter, president of Save the Bankhead and Bothwell, helped arrange for the city to take ownership of the theater and the debt. The arrangement allowed LVPAC to lease and manage the theater. The City of San Francisco trucks its trash through Livermore to a facility on the Altamont. They pay Livermore a trash mitigation fee per truck for the privilege. These funds were used for the bank payments, requiring no city tax funds. The Bothwell lease was continued, and the entire big theater development project was ended.[20] LVPAC's activities caused some to consider it a political action committee both in name and deed. Consequently, the organization was renamed Livermore Valley Arts. The failure of the regional theater plan reopened discussion for the non-housing segment of the former station site. Disparate concepts included moving the housing elsewhere with divided public opinion between a large park or a large hotel and conference facility. The city proposed a compromise with the Stockman's Association and the commitment to the housing commission, to build housing on a portion of the site. The Stockman's Association supported the development of a limited Veterans Park and also constructed a statue commemorating those who replaced their cowboy hats for military helmets in World War I. Veterans Statue in Veterans Park was completed in 2020.

The new senior facility which replaced the Bothwell Center, had been used for senior lunch services, community events and classes. The Bothwell is now used for art and music lessons and small theatrical presentations. The artist studios were leased by LVPAC. The large room is a bit larger than the Bankhead Theater stage and is the rehearsal venue for the opera company and occasionally for the symphony and the Pleasanton Band.

The redevelopment of First Street had been a long-time goal of the city. The plan was to decrease through automobile and truck traffic, reduce lanes, add diagonal parking, and generate wider, tree-lined sidewalks. These changes were not possible while it was a state highway. The state's redesignation of Highway 84 to Isabel Avenue as and its opening as an expressway ended the state's limitations of the First Street redevelopment in 2012.

Parking improvement became a planning priority especially after the opening of the ACE station. Initially, a temporary parking lot was established on the former railroad station property east of Livermore Avenue. The city delayed building the Bankhead Theater and other development on that property until a multi-story parking garage, across Railroad Avenue, was completed.

Livermore's sister city relationships began in 1965 with Quetzaltenango, Guatemala, and Yotsukaido, Japan, in 1977. The relationship between the Lab and similar Russian institutions began to open up after the fall of the Soviet Union. Snezhinsk had been a closed laboratory city and was visited by U.S. scientists. Livermore Mayor Cathie Brown, members of the Rotary Club, and the Lab proposed creating a sister city relationship. It was established with the approval and support of the Department of Energy. It became part of the program to limit nuclear weapons. The relationship opened the door to mutual visits by Brown and members of the Lab with leaders of Snezhinsk. The relationship faltered with a new mayor and city council as well as changing Russian political positions.[21]

A movie produced in 2002 by Rachel Ramey and David Murray, featured several uniquely Livermore events and garnered national attention.[22] The film included excerpts of photographer Bill Owens' book *Suburbia*, the lost time capsule, the totem pole curse, as well as establishment of the sister city of Snezhinsk, and the light bulb anniversary celebration.

Livermorium, element 116, was named for Livermore. It was synthesized by Livermore Lab scientists at the Joint Institute of Nuclear

Veterans Statue in Veterans Park was completed in 2020. The park area is still under construction. (*Author's photo*)

Research Dubna Russia (JINR). Oak Ridge National Laboratory, Vanderbilt University, and the University of Nevada, Las Vegas, scientists also participated in the discovery. Livermorium is one of six new heavy elements discovered by the Dubna-Livermore team.[23]

There was a long-time gas station on the southeast corner of Mills Square at First Street and Livermore Avenue. The gas station was one of the first established in the town and had severely contaminated the ground. The city acquired the site after the gas station closed. It became an unofficial plaza with several picnic tables. Mayor John Marchand and city council decided to develop the plaza to celebrate the Livermorium discovery. Nothing had been done about the contamination, and the state required the site be decontaminated before anything could be built. The state ruled the entity that created contamination was responsible for the clean up. Chevron was notified, but claimed the city was responsible since they owned the property. The council rejected Chevron's claim when the mayor, who was also a chemist, noted the contamination was lead and hydrocarbons and went into the ground 20 feet. Chevron agreed to underwrite the clean up, though a spokesperson later admitted they just wanted to pave it over.

The city's Commission for the Arts invited designs for the plaza, and three were presented to the public for approval. Each of the three designs was approved by 30 percent of those responding. The design chosen by the council had the best combination of art and science, and it also represented a strong connection between the city and the Lab. It features a floating 18,000-pound granite sphere representing the nucleus of the atom which is easily rotated by small children. The council defined the plaza address to be 116 South Livermore Avenue, appropriate because the address of Peet's Coffee is 152 South and the corner is 100 South.

The Collings Foundation's Living History Display of Aircraft annually flew into Livermore airport around Memorial Day. The foundation's aircraft included the Boeing B-17 Flying Fortress *Nine O Nine*, Consolidated B-24 Liberator *Witchcraft*, and North American P-51C Mustang *Betty Jane*. Local World War II veterans and restored aircraft also joined the fly in. Local citizens had the opportunity to visit, explore, and ride these unique and rare treasures of aviation history.[24] The annual events ended after the tragic 2019 crash of the *Nine O Nine*.[25]

First Street redevelopment was successful in making the downtown attractive to the public, it also created significant parking limitations. The city paved and formed a temporary parking area on the former train station site between Livermore Avenue and L Street. That lot was often filled because of the multiple restaurants and shops on redeveloped portions of First Street. That lot remained important while the city's plan for the station site was being discussed. Parking plans evolved for the recently completed Railroad Avenue Garage at I Street. The station site lot was to include a new multi-story garage at the L Street end of the site. Major construction of the L Street garage is underway and should be completed in 2025. Construction on the majority of the site is being delayed until a lawsuit is resolved. The suit is attempting to remove housing from the site to build a large conference center. The redevelopment of First Street is ongoing. An important aspect of the redevelopment is the preservation of historic structures in the older part of downtown.

Shakespeare & Performing Arts Regional Company (SPARC), formerly known as Livermore Shakespeare Theater, has for twenty years been putting on small, high-quality theatrical productions. Without their own theater, their presentations have been presented in vineyards, public arts venues, and schools.

The Quest Science Center was formed and run by Livermore Lab retirees, employees, and educators that create activities for students and the next generation of innovators and problem solvers. Through the past several years, they have been hosting a series of well-attended outdoor science events for children.

The city's plans reserved sites for a small black box theater for SPARC and a science education center for Quest on the former station site. They retained the original plan for the smaller boutique hotel on the east side of Livermore Avenue. Both SPARC and Quest are raising funds and have city-approved plans to construct facilities adjacent to Stockman's Park.

The number of employees at the labs peaked at more than 10,000 during the nuclear arms race. It then declined more than 30 percent after the demise of the Soviet Union. The hiring was limited after the contract with the University of California was changed from a non-profit to a for-profit with private industry in 2007. The labs now represent a smaller segment of the city's population. However, their high-level technical presence continues to support science education, create spin-off companies and attract others to locate here.

The rising cost of housing with only limited rises in salaries has forced many workers to live and commute from less expensive areas. These include lower-wage teachers, restaurant employees, and city and district workers, including staff, police, and fire department personnel. Several projects and city ordinances are expanding housing reserved for lower-wage employees. The police department has also assembled a team to help refer the unhoused to local services.

Valley Memorial Hospital became Valley Care and purchased a 23-acre parcel of land in Pleasanton to build what would become one of the valley's main medical center and hospital campus in 1991. Stanford Health Care and Valley Care merged twenty-five years later. Kaiser and other medical conglomerates also developed a presence in the valley in recent years. Increasing cost of medical services and insurance have limited treatment for lower-wage residents. Axis Community Health was organized to provide care to lower-income valley residents regardless of insurance or lack thereof. Axis is supported by local Rotary, state and federal funding, foundation grants, and limited patient fees.

Las Positas College has opened both non-academic and advanced academic classes to high school students. Because of such activities Las Positas is currently rated as the best community college in the state.[26]

Randy Johnson was one of the few exceptional sportsmen to graduate from Livermore High School. He pitched a perfect game in his senior year and went on to pitch in the major leagues for twenty-two years. He played with seven teams including the San Francisco Giants. He pitched no hitters in both leagues and won the Cy Young Award five times. He was elected to the Baseball Hall of Fame in 2015.

Livermore native Matt Finders, formerly a musician in Johnny Carson's band, returned to the city and organized The Element 116 Jazz Band for high school students. They play at local events including intermissions of resident company's shows at the Bankhead Theater and are well regarded.

The local weekly paper *Livermore Independent* concentrates on the major valley issues. It is still going strong as a small, weekly, free, local paper after more than fifty years. Two local news sites are currently available online. They include the *Livermore Patch* and the *Livermore Vine*.

Change and expansion of the city continues unabated. With increasing population and the greater time requirements for making a living and commuting, residents are only able to spend limited time on local activities. A noticeable aspect is that it has become less likely for impromptu social interactions at the grocery or on the street, unlike fifty years ago.

The population of Livermore was nearly constant from only a few years after its founding until about 1950. The population boom was initially created by the Lab and then followed by the interstate freeway commuters. Each of the groups had significantly different sociological and financial interests, often reflected by the actions of boards of directors of the city and tax districts. The differing interests are weekly evident in the letters to the editor of the *Livermore Independent Newspaper*.

The interests of the historic citizens were developing a financially viable and functional city. They later supported and led rapid, virtually uncontrolled development. The Lab-based population grew to about 40,000 and is now diminishing. They redirected the interest of the city to controlled development, improved parks, education, arts, and historic preservation. The commuters generally support the development of sporting facilities and activities for their children.

The population of Livermore is now about 90,000 with the large numbers of commuters. The good news is that the city's finances are thriving. The downtown, the scientific and arts communities, parks, and sporting facilities are also doing well.

This modern mural on the side of a building at the entrance to downtown is one of several murals by Livermore artists that were painted during the pandemic. The artists who painted this mural include Owen Matthew Aurelio, Jami Butler, Thomasin Dewhurst, John Ernst, Anne Giancola, Ozell Hudson, Caren Kreger, Vera Lowdermilk, Joel Salinas III, and Elliot Thompson. (*Author's photo*)

ENDNOTES

Chapter 1

1 Margolin, *The Ohlone Way* (1978).

2 Boilton (Editor), *Diary of Fray Juan Crespi, in Palou's Historical Memoirs of New California, Vol. 2* (1927), p. 48.

3 www.muwekma.org/.

4 Cook, *The Aboriginal Population of Alameda & Contra Costa Counties, California* (2022), pp. 30-31.

5 *Ibid.*, pp. 40-41.

6 Engelhardt, *The Missions and Missionaries of California* (1915), p. 37.

7 Cook, *op. cit.*, pp. 30-31, 37.

8 Thompson and West, *Historical Atlas of Alameda County* (1878), p. 163.

9 Newton, *Las Positas* (1969), p. 66.

10 Homan, *Historic Livermore, California, Illustrated, A–Z* (2007), p. 58.

11 Newton, *op. cit.*, pp. 71-72.

12 *Ibid.*, p. 80.

13 Homan, *op. cit.*, p. 293.

14 Wood, *History of Alameda County* (1883), p. 461.

15 Homan, *op. cit.*, p. 293.

16 Wood, *op. cit.*, p. 461.

17 Livermore Heritage Guild, *The Story of William M. Mendenhall, Founder of the Town of Livermore* p. 1-4.

18 Wood, *op. cit.*, p. 172.

19 Johnston-Dodds, *Early California Laws and Policies Related to California Indians* (2002), p. 21.

20 *Ibid.*, pp. 40-41.

21 Brewer, *Up and Down California, Fourth Edition* (2003).

22 Bryant, *What I Saw in California* (1848).

23 Hittell, *The Adventures of James Capen Adams, Mountaineer and Grizzly Bear Hunter, of California* (1911).

24 County of Alameda, California, *Easement* (1855).

25 Mosier and Williams, *History of Tesla, A California Coal Mining Town* (1998 and 2002), p. 7.

26 Wood, *op. cit.*, p. 464.

27 Livermore Heritage Guild, *Map of Murray Township* (1874).

Chapter 2

1 Bain, *Empire Express* (1999); and Ambrose, *Nothing like It In the World* (2000).

2 Bain, *op. cit.*, pp. 19-46.

3 32nd Congress, *Chapter 143*, March 3, 1853.

4 U.S. War Department, *Reports of Explorations and Surveys, to Ascertain the Most Practicable and Economical Route for a Railroad from the Mississippi River to the Pacific Ocean, Vol. 5, Pt. 1 (1855–60)*, pp. 11-13.

5 National Archives, *Pacific Railroad Survey* (1853).

6 Bain, *op. cit.*, pp. 52-53.

7 Judah, *A Practical Plan for Building the Pacific Railroad* (1857).

8 Tutorow, *The Governor* (2004), pp. 182-191.

9 *Ibid.*, p. 121.

10 The Pony Express (1860).

11 Bain, *op. cit.*, p. 83.

12 Lavender, *The Great Persuader* (1970), p. 97.

13 *Ibid.*, p. 98

14 Tutorow, *op. cit.*, pp. 192-204.

15 *Ibid.*, p. 214.

16 Lavender, *op. cit.*, pp. 121-122.

17 United States 37th Congress, *Chapter CXX*, July 1, 1862.

18 United States 38th Congress, *Chapter CCXVI*, July 2, 1864.

19 Bain, *op. cit.*, pp. 127-128.

20 *Sacramento Daily Union*, April 15, 1863, p. 2.

21 Tutorow, *op. cit.*, p. 259.

22 *Daily Alta California*, May 27, 1863, p. 1.

23 Hees, *E-Mail Communication with Author*, April 30, 2009.

24 Ping-Chiu, *Chinese Labor in California, 1850–1880: An Economic Study* (1963), p. 41.

25 Bain, *op. cit.*, p. 207.

26 *Daily Alta California*, May 29, 1867, p. 1; May 29, 1867, p. 1.

27 Bain, *op. cit.*, p. 336.

28 Tutorow, *op. cit.*, p. 266.

29 *Stockton Independent*, June 5, 1867, p. 2.

30 Tutorow, *op. cit.*, pp. 260-264.

31 Robertson, *Encyclopedia of Western Railroad History, Vol. 5* (1998), p. 296.

32 *Daily Alta California*, March 7, 1868, p. 2.

33 Lavender, *op. cit.*, p. 174.

34 *Ibid.*, p. 186.

35 Robertson, *Encyclopedia of Western Railroad History, Vol. 5* (1998), Vol. 5, p. 296.

36 Bain, *op. cit.*, p. 710.

37 Lavender, *op. cit.*, p. 292.

38 Tutorow, *op. cit.*, p. 342.

39 Myrick, *Western Pacific (WPRY of 1910), The Last Transcontinental Railroad, Colorado Rail Annual No. 27* (2006), pp. 23-36.

40 *San Jose Mercury-News*, March 19, 1868, p. 2.

41 *Sacramento Daily Union*, June 5, 1869, p. 5.

42 *Ibid.*, May 3, 1869, p. 8.

43 *Ibid.*, February 9, 1869, p. 3.

44 *Ibid.*, April 2, 1869, p. 3.

45 *Ibid.*, June 15, 1869, p. 3.

46 *San Jose Mercury-News*, August 4, 1869, p. 2.

47 *Sacramento Daily Union*, August 19, 1869, p. 2.

48 *Stockton Independent*, September 6, 1869, p. 3.

49 *Sacramento Daily Union*, September 7, 1869, p. 2.

50 Signor, *Southern Pacific's Western Division* (2003), p. 23.

51 Low and Becker, *Some Reflections of an Early California Governor* (1883), p. 39.

Chapter 3

1 Wood, *History of Alameda County* (1883), p. 468.

2 *Ibid.*, p. 469.

3 Homan, *Historic Livermore, California, Illustrated, A–Z* (2007), pp. 269-271.

4 *Sacramento Daily Union*, March 10, 1869, p. 2. Reprinted from *Alameda County Gazette*, March 6, 1869.

5 Wood, *op. cit.*, p. 350.

6 Wood, *A Summary of Criminal History of Alameda County from 1853 to 1881, Many of which were in and around Laddsville and Livermore*, pp. 336-371.

7 *Daily Alta California*, July 30, 1870, p. 2.

8 *Daily Evening Herald (Stockton)*, September 27, 1871, p. 1.

9 *Livermore Herald*, March 31, 1917, p. 1.

10 Homan, *op. cit.*, p. 367.

11 Livermore Heritage Guild, *The Story of William M. Mendenhall, Founder of the Town of Livermore*, p. 4.

12 Livermore Heritage Guild, *Map of Murray Township, Alameda County* (1874).

13 *San Jose Mercury-News*, November 5, 1869, p. 2.

14 *Ibid.*, October 17, 1873, p. 1.

15 *Ibid.*, p. 203.

16 LeConte, *A Journal of Ramblings* (1960), p. 3.

17 Central Pacific Railroad, timetable, October 18, 1869.

18 Alameda County, *Grant Deed from SP Transportation Co. to SP Land Co. Alameda County 74-91689, May 21, 1974; Alameda County, May 11, 1870; Liber 55 of Deeds, p. 50; March 18,1871, Liber 64 of Deeds*, p. 340.

19 Kaskey and Finn, *Livermore Heritage Guild* (2009).

20 Wood, *op. cit.* (1883), p. 469 cites 20 acres; p. 942 cites 32 acres.

21 *Stockton Independent*, January 22, 1869, p. 3.

22 *Livermore Enterprise*, September 11, 1875, p. 3.

23 Bender, Jr., *Southern Pacific Lines Standard Design Depots*, (2013), p. 25; and *Map of Murray Township, op. cit.*

24 Homan, *Ice* (2007), pp. 249-250.

25 *Livermore Enterprise*, July 15, 1876, p. 3.

26 *Ibid.*, November 4, 1876, p. 3.

27 Frank, *Depot*, Livermore Heritage Guild (2019), p. 21.

28 *Daily Alta California*, December 6, 1869, p. 2.

29 *Stockton Independent*, November 28, 1872, p. 2.

30 Bronzan, *A Historical Study of the Livermore Valley Joint Unified School District* (1973), p. 19.

31 *Livermore Enterprise*, May 30, 1874, p. 3; June 13, 1874.

32 *Ibid.*, June 15, 1876, p. 3.

33 *California State Gazetteer and Business Directory* (1888), p. 382.

34 *Livermore Herald*, April 16, 2004, p. 1.

35 *Livermore Enterprise*, September 2, 1876, p. 3.

36 Kleineke and Drummond, *125 Years, A History of the First Presbyterian Church, Livermore, California* (1955).

37 Nebo, William, *In Person Communication with Author* (2024).

38 Town Council, minutes, June 10, 1882.

39 *Stockton Independent*, May 28, 1870, p. 2.

40 *Sonoma Democrat*, June 4, 1870, p. 8.

41 *Sacramento Daily Union*, January 13, 1871, p. 3.

42 *Ibid.*, February 17, 1871, p. 2.

43 *Stockton Independent*, September 19, 1871, p. 2.

44 *Ibid.*, November 28, 1872.

45 Homan, *Historic Livermore, California, Illustrated, A–Z* (2007), p. 21-22.

46 *Stockton Independent*, July 7, 1871, p. 3.

47 *San Jose Mercury-News*, September 4, 1873, p. 2.

48 Town Council, minutes, September 18, 1876.

49 Homan, *op. cit.*, pp. 501-503.

50 *San Jose Mercury-News*, December 1, 1872, p. 2.

51 *Ibid.*, February 16, 1870, p. 2.

52 *Marysville Daily Appeal*, February 18, 1872, p. 1; Reprinted from the *Oakland Transcript*, February 12, 1872.

53 *Daily Alta California*, September 4, 1873, p. 1.

54 *Sacramento Daily Union*, February 19, 1873, p. 3.

55 *Daily Alta California*, March 1, 1869, p. 3.

56 *Sacramento Daily Union*, July 9, 1869, p. 16.

57 *Stockton Independent*, May 26, 1870, p. 2.

58 *Livermore Enterprise*, May 22, 1875, p. 3.

59 *Ibid.*, December 4, 1875, p. 2.

60 Livermore Heritage Guild, *Map of Murray Township in Eastern Alameda County* (1874).

61 *Livermore Enterprise*, June 27, 1874, p. 2.

62 *San Francisco Chronicle*, December 30, 1873; July 18, 1875.

63 *New York Times and San Francisco Chronicle*, December 14, 1883, p. 1.

64 *San Francisco Chronicle*, January 6, 1884, p. 1.

65 *Ibid.*, April 24, 1895, p. 1.

66 *Livermore Enterprise*, July 17, 1875, p. 3.

67 *Ibid.*, April 3, 1875, p. 3.

68 *Livermore Herald*, June 26, 1942, p. 1.

69 *Ibid.*, September 27, 1929, p. 8.

70 *Sacramento Daily Union*, June 6, 1872, p. 3.

71 *San Jose Mercury-News*, August 12, 1873, p. 3.

72 Homan, *op. cit.*, p. 45.

73 *Ibid.*, p. 361.

74 *Livermore Herald*, March 3, 1877, p. 1.

75 *Livermore Echo*, December 30, 1897, p. 3.

76 *Ibid.*, December 24, 1896, p. 3.

77 *Ibid.*, June 21, 1894, p. 3.

78 *Livermore Herald*, September 22, 1881, p. 3.

79 *Ibid.*, July 2, 1879, p. 4.
80 *Livermore Enterprise*, December 11, 1875, p. 2.
81 *Ibid.*, January 22, 1876, p. 2.
82 Homan, *op. cit.*, p. 282.
83 Halley, *Centennial Yearbook of Alameda County, Oakland* (1876).

Chapter 4

1 *Livermore Enterprise*, April 15, 1876, p. 2.
2 *Ibid.*, May 18, 1876, p. 2.
3 Halley, *Centennial Yearbook of Alameda County, Oakland* (1876).
4 Livermore Board of Trustees, minutes, May 15 and 18, 1876.
5 *Livermore Enterprise*, June 3, 1876, p. 3.
6 Livermore Board of Trustees, minutes, June 1876.
7 Livermore Heritage Guild, Chapters of Livermore, Livermore Town Halls.
8 *Livermore Herald*, November 25, 1911, 1.3.
9 *Ibid.*, March 28, 1903, p. 5.
10 *Livermore Enterprise*, April 10, 1875, p. 3.
11 *Ibid.*, August 5, 1876, p. 2.
12 Homan, *Historic Livermore, California, Illustrated, A–Z* (2007), p. 305.
13 Livermore Board of Trustees, minutes, September 11, 1876
14 Jensen, John "Jack," recorded interview, Livermore Heritage Guild, May 12, 1981.
15 *Livermore Enterprise*, September 9, 1876, p. 2.
16 Livermore Board of Trustees, minutes, May 17, 1879.
17 *Stockton Independent*, October 30, 1873, p. 2.
18 Livermore Board of Trustees, minutes, March 21, 1887.
19 *Livermore Enterprise*, July 15, 1876, p. 3.
20 Advertisements in multiple issues of the *Livermore Enterprise*.
21 *Livermore Echo*, June 8, 1905, p. 3.
22 Homan, *op. cit.*, pp. 298-300.
23 *Livermore Herald*, March 28, 1877, p. 4.
24 *Livermore Enterprise*, December 16, 1876, p. 3.
25 Wood, *History of Alameda County* (1883), p. 930.
26 Jensen, John "Jack," recorded interview, Livermore Heritage Guild, May 12, 1981.
27 *Livermore Echo*, January 1, 1891, p. 3.
28 *Livermore Enterprise*, May 23, 1874, p. 3.
29 *Livermore Echo*, November 8, 1889, p. 3.
30 *Ibid.*, May 3, 1888, p. 3.
31 *Ibid.*, February 11, 1897, p. 2.
32 *Livermore Enterprise*, June 26, 1875, p. 2.
33 *Ibid.*, April 3, 1875 p. 2; December 11, 1875, p.3.
34 *Ibid.*, November 20, 1875, p. 3.
35 Livermore Board of Trustees, minutes, May 18, 1876.
36 *Ibid.*, July 13, 1878.
37 Town of Livermore, Ordinance No. 45, February 7, 1881.
38 Livermore Board of Trustees, minutes, April 4, 1881.
39 *Ibid.*, May 15, 1882.
40 *Livermore Echo*, December 27, 1894, p. 3.

41 *Livermore Enterprise*, June 13, 1874, p. 2.

42 *Livermore Herald*, May 25, 1912, p. 1.

43 Livermore Board of Trustees, minutes, July 11, 1881.

44 *Livermore Echo*, May 28, 1896, p. 3

45 *Ibid.*, February 25, 1897, p. 3.

46 *Livermore Herald*, October 21, 1911, p. 7.

47 Mitchel, *Reports on Multiple Dates in the Livermore Enterprise* (1875–1876).

48 *Livermore Echo*, January 23, 1880, p. 3.

49 Homan, *op. cit.*, pp. 96-97.

50 *Livermore Enterprise*, August 4, 1874, p. 2.

51 *Ibid.*, April 24, 1875, p. 2.

52 *Ibid.*, April 1, 1876, p. 3.

53 Town of Livermore, Ordinance No. 45, February 7, 1881.

54 *Livermore Herald*, January 1, 1879, p. 3.

55 Tutorow, *The Governor, The Life and Legacy of Leland Stanford* (2004), p. 389.

56 Cottrell, *It took 92 Years for California to Ratify the 15th Amendment*, *The Union* (Grass Valley, California), June 26, 2020.

57 *Livermore Herald*, May 26, 1881, p. 2.

58 *Ibid.*, June 1, 1882, p. 4.

59 *Ibid.*, June 1, 1882, p. 1.

60 Concannon, telephone conversation with author (2023).

61 *Livermore Echo and Herald*, various dates between 1889 and 1904.

62 *Livermore Herald*, June 20, 1889, p. 2.

63 *Ibid.*, May 6, 1899, p. 3.

64 Homan, *op. cit.*, p. 513.

65 *Livermore Herald*, March 24, 1887, p. 2; reprinted from *San Francisco Chronicle*, March 21, 1887.

66 *Livermore Herald*, July 27, 1882, p. 3.

67 *Ibid.*, December 8 and 22, 1881, p. 3.

68 Young, Livermore Heritage Guild, Chapters of Livermore, Altamont Barbed Wire Telephone Company (1980).

69 *Livermore Echo*, December 13, 1888, p. 3.

70 *Ibid.*, October 12, 1905, p. 3.

71 *Ibid.*, July 3, 1890, p. 3; *Echo*, 3 July 1890, p. 3.

72 *San Francisco Chronicle*, July 6, 1870.

73 Burnham, *History & Geology of Livermore Oil* (2018), pp. 35-64.

74 *Pacific Rural Press*, March 18, 1881, p. 167.

75 Livermore Trustee Council, minutes, November 2, 1885.

76 Homan, *op. cit.*, pp. 44-46.

77 *Livermore Echo*, July 2, 1891, p. 3.

78 Lemos, in-person communication with author, February 27, 2016.

79 Guild, Livermore Heritage, Sanborn Insurance Maps (1907), p. 10.

80 Homan, *op. cit.*, pp. 285 and 289.

81 Mauch, The Livermore College, Chapters of Livermore, Livermore Heritage Guild.

82 Bronzan, *A Historical Study of the Livermore Valley Joint Unified School District*, (1973), pp. 33-34, 86.

83 *Ibid.*, pp. 45-46, 87.

84 *Sacramento Daily Union*, July 14, 1894, p. 2.

85 Bancroft, *The Native Races* (1883).

86 *San Francisco Examiner*, August 27, 1899.

87 Gifford, *Miwok Cults* (1926).

88 *Livermore Echo*, August 3, 1899, p. 3.

89 *Livermore Herald*, editorial, October 11, 1919, p. 8.

Chapter 5

1 *Sacramento Daily Union*, December 23, 1869, p. 2.; *Stockton Independent*, December 16, 1869, p. 2.

2 *Stockton Independent*, May 3, 1870, p. 3.

3 Evans, *Collis Potter Huntington* (1954), pp. 299-321.

4 *Daily Alta California*, September 7, 1869, p. 2.; September 8, 1869, p. 4.

5 *Ibid.*, September 7, 1869, p. 2.; September 8, 1869, p. 4.

6 Rayner, *The Associates*, (2008), p. 110; Lavender, *The Great Persuader*, (1970), p. 292.

7 Tutorow, *The Governor* (2004), p. 342.

8 Klein, *The Life & Legend of Jay Gould* (1985), pp. 139-141.

9 Lavender, *The Great Persuader* (1970), pp. 293-295.

10 Tutorow, *op. cit.*, pp. 268-270.

11 *Sacramento Daily Union*, November 25, 1869, p. 2.

12 *Daily Alta California*, November 15, 1869, p. 1.

13 *Sacramento Daily Union*, December 1, 1869, p. 3

14 *Ibid.*, October 26, 1870, p. 2.

15 *Stockton Independent*, October 25, 1869, p. 3.

16 *Ibid.*, October 29, 1869, p. 3.

17 *Ibid.*, October 25, 1869, p. 3.

18 Janney, *United States Patent, Nos. 138 and 405*, April 29, 1873.

19 Westinghouse, *United States Patent, Nos. 88 and 929*, April 13, 1869.

20 Lavender, *op. cit.*, p. 186.

21 *Ibid.*, p. 286.

22 Signor, *Southern Pacific's Western Division* (2003), pp. 36-38.

23 Robertson, *Encyclopedia of Western Railroad History, Vol. 4, California* (1998), pp. 100-105.

24 Tutorow, *op. cit.*, pp. 812-906; and Orsi, *Sunset Limited* (2005) pp. 92-103.

25 *Grass Valley Daily Union*, October 24, 1884, p. 3.

26 White, *Railroaded: The Transcontinentals and The Making of Modern America* (2011), pp. 429-450.

27 Lavender, *op. cit.*, p. 243.

28 *Ibid.*, p. 271 and 362.

29 McCullough, *The Path Between the Seas* (1977), pp. 275 and 609.

30 Tutorow, *op. cit.*, pp. 812-906.

31 Morgenthau, *All in a Lifetime* (1922), p. 73.

32 White, *op. cit.*, pp. 398-409.

33 Signor, *op. cit.*, p. 43.

34 Klein, *Union Pacific, Vol. 2, 1894–1969* (2006), pp. 155-157.

35 *Livermore Herald*, December 27. 1902, p. 1.

36 Hiltzik, *Iron Empires* (2020), pp. 361 and 371.

37 Norris, *The Octopus* (1901).

38 Klein, *op. cit.*, p. 181.

39 *Livermore Herald*, January 5, 1882, p. 3.; February 9, 1882, p. 2.

40 Fickewirth, *California Railroads* (1992), p. 23.

41 Mosier and Williams, *History of Tesla, A California Coal Mining Town* (2002), pp. 31, 52-57.

42 *Livermore Herald*, January 9, 1897, p. 2.

43 Hiltzik, *op. cit.*, pp. 361 and 371.

44 Fickewirth, *op. cit.*, p. 164.

45 Myrick, *Western Pacific, The Last Transcontinental Railroad, Colorado Rail Annual No. 27* (2006), pp. 23-36.

46 Klein, *op. cit.*, pp. 150-152.

47 Gould, *The Presidency of Theodore Roosevelt* (2012), pp. 37-38, 45-47.

48 51st Congress, Session 1, *Chapter 647*, July 2, 1890.

49 Orsi, *Sunset Limited* (2005) p. 33.

50 Robertson, *op. cit.*, p. 243.

51 Livermore Trustees, minutes, January 2, 1906.

52 *Ibid.*

53 *Livermore Herald*, February 6, 1904, p. 1.

54 *Ibid.*, March 19, 1904, p. 4.

55 Southern Pacific, *Livermore Station Plans*, California Sate Railroad Museum (Files LS 64/1 and 2).

56 *Livermore Herald*, March 17, 1906, p. 2; August 2, 1913, p. 1.

57 *Livermore Journal*, January 25, 1924, p. 2.

58 *Livermore Herald*, November 25, 1925, p. 1.

59 *Ibid.*, October 10, 1930, p. 1; November 7, 1930, p. 4.

60 Stover, *Historical Atlas of the American Railroads*, (1999), p. 2.

61 Klein, *op. cit.*, pp. 227-239.

62 *Livermore Herald*, 26 July 26, 1919, p. 1.

63 Oliver, *James J. Hill: Transforming the American Northwest* (2001).

64 DeNevi, *The Western Pacific* (1978), p. 75.

65 *Livermore Journal*, December 12, 1929, p. 1.

66 *Ibid.*, June 1, 1928, p. 1.

67 *Ibid.*, June 1, 1928, p. 8.

68 *Ibid.*, January 18, 1928, p. 1.

69 *Ibid.*, May 31, 1928, p. 1.

70 *Livermore Herald*, October 31, 1924, p. 8.

71 *Ibid.*, August 5, 1927, p. 1.

72 *Ibid.*, May 11, 1923, p. 1.

73 *Ibid.*, June 18,1921, p. 4.

74 Mosier and Williams, *op. cit.*, p. 313.

Chapter 6

1 *Livermore Herald*, January 6, 1910, p. 6.

2 *Livermore Echo*, May 14, 1903, p. 3.

3 Bunshah, *Company Eye, The Old Guard*, Livermore Heritage Guild, Chapters of Livermore.

4 Henry, *History & Roster of Company Eye* (1967).

5 *Livermore Herald*, May 9, 1947, p. 1.

6 Eberly, Dottie, personal conversation with the author, February 17, 2016.

7 *Livermore Herald*, April 16, 1910, p. 2.

8 *Livermore Echo*, May 28, 1896, p. 3.

9 *Ibid.*, February 25, 1897, p. 3.

10 *Los Angeles Herald*, May 26, 1901, p. 5.

11 Wood, *History of Alameda County* (1883), p. 930.

12 *Livermore Herald*, April 5, 1916: p. 1.

13 Jensen, John "Jack," recorded interview, Livermore Heritage Guild, May 12, 1981.

14 *Ibid.*

15 Hagemann, Herbert, oral history transcript, Livermore Heritage Guild (1985), p. 9.

16 *Livermore Echo*, September 5, 1905, p. 2.

17 Livermore Town Halls, Chapters of Livermore, Livermore Heritage Guild.

18 Homan, *Historic Livermore, California, Illustrated, A–Z* (2007), pp. 450-453.

19 *Livermore Herald*, April 16, 1904, p. 1.

20 *Livermore Echo*, June 25, 1908, p. 1.

21 *Livermore Herald*, November 12, 1948, p. 1.

22 *Livermore Herald*, February 13, 1904.

23 *Ibid.*, May 4, 1907, p. 1.

24 *Ibid.*, August 9, 1919, p. 1.

25 *Ibid.*, August 22, 1908, p. 1.

26 *Ibid.*, December 27, 1913, p. 1.

27 *Ibid.*, July 5, 1929, p. 2.

28 *Ibid.*, January 1, 1932, p. 1.

29 Homan, *op. cit.*, p. 492.

30 *Livermore Herald*, April 20, 1923, p. 1.

31 *Ibid.*, April 11, 1924, p. 3.

32 *Ibid.*, July 29, 1899, p. 6.

33 *Livermore Herald*, July 14, 1900, p. 1.

34 *Ibid.*, February 16, 1901, p. 1.

35 *Ibid.*, September 27, 1902, p. 1.

36 *Ibid.*, March 14, 1903, p. 2.

37 *Ibid.*, June 27, 1903, p. 5.

38 *Livermore Echo*, October 20, 1904, p. 3.

39 *Ibid.*, September 17, 1903, p. 3.

40 *Ibid.*, January 24, 1907, p. 1.

41 *Livermore Herald*, September 26, 1903, p. 3.

42 *Ibid.*, May 9, 1914, p. 1.

43 *Ibid.*, October 20, 1906, p. 1.

44 *Ibid.*, May 17, 1902, p. 2.

45 *Ibid.*, March 30, 1912, p. 6.

46 *Ibid.*, April 17, 1915, p. 1.

47 *Ibid.*, August 7, 1915, p. 8.

48 *Ibid.*, May 23, 1924, p. 8.

49 *Ibid.*, March 11, 1927, p. 8.

50 *Livermore Echo*, April 16, 1908, p. 1.

51 *Ibid.*, December 9, 1909, p. 4.

52 *Livermore Herald, Greatest Calamity of Modern Times*, April 21, 1906, p. 1.

53 *Ibid.*, August 4, 1906, p. 3.

54 *Ibid.*, Aprel 19, 1906, p. 3.

55 *Ibid.*, April 28, 1906, p. 1.; *Livermore Echo*, April 26, 1906.

56 Livermore Trustees, minutes, January 2, 1906.

57 Homan, *op. cit.*, p. 418.

58 *Livermore Herald*, March 14, 1908, p. 3 and May 30, 1908, p. 1.

59 Jensen, John "Jack," recorded interview, Livermore Heritage Guild,
    May 12, 1981.
60 *Livermore Herald*, September 6, 1919, p. 1.
61 Homan, *op. cit.*, p. 226; *Livermore Echo*, Multiple Articles, Summer 1911.
62 Southern Pacific, Livermore Station Plans, 1926–1959.
63 *Livermore Herald*, January 8, 1923, p. 1.
64 *Ibid.*, August 6, 1921, pp. 2 and 8.
65 *Ibid.*, September 7, 1923, p. 1.
66 *Ibid.*, July 17 and 24, 1915, p. 1.
67 Schrader, *Will the Last Person Leaving Livermore Please Unscrew the Bulb In
    Fire Station One* (1990), p. 11.
68 Jensen, John "Jack," recorded interview, Livermore Heritage Guild,
    May 12, 1981.
69 *Livermore Herald*, July 20, 1928, p. 5.
70 Laughlin and McGlinchey, *Livermore Rodeo History* (1993).
71 Szmyd, personal communication with author (2024).
72 Rasmussen, personal communication with author (2024).
73 *Livermore Herald*, November 23, 1901, p. 2.
74 *Ibid.*, August 10, 1923, p. 1.
75 *Ibid.*, August 22, 1924, p. 8.; September 5, 1924, p. 3.
76 *Ibid.*, January 16, 1925, p. 1.
77 *Ibid.*, January 12, 1918, p. 1.
78 *Ibid.*, February 3, 1917, p. 4.
79 *Ibid.*, March 10, 1917, p. 8.
80 *Ibid.*, April 20, 1923, p. 1.
81 *Ibid.*, October 1, 1910, p. 1.
82 Mosier, *Brick Making in the Livermore Valley* (2001).
83 *Livermore Journal*, January 5, 1927, p. 1.
84 *Livermore Echo*, August 1893, p. 3.
85 Mauch, Livermore College, Chapters of Livermore, Livermore Heritage Guild.
86 *Livermore Herald*, August 26, 1960, p. 8.
87 Devnich, *Livermore Medicine in the Old Days* (2003).
88 *Livermore Herald*, April 17, 1925, p. 1.
89 *Ibid.*, June 10, 1927, p. 1.
90 *Ibid.*, April 11, 1903, p. 1.
91 *Ibid.*, October 28, 1909, and December 30, 1909, p. 4.
92 *Ibid.*, May 25, 1912, p. 1.
94 *Livermore Herald*, August 23, 1919, p. 1.
95 *Ibid.*, October 11, 1919, p. 8.
96 *Ibid.*, July 22, 1927, p. 1.
97 "Save Mount Diablo," Eye of Diablo Press Release, April 10, 2020.
98 *Livermore Journal*, December 18, 1926, p. 1.
99 Livermore Board of Trustees, minutes, July 21, 1924.
100 *Livermore Journal*, November 21, 1924, p. 1; December 5, 9, 1924, p. 1.
101 *Livermore Herald*, July 20, 1928, p. 5.
102 Withers, *The President Travels By Train* (1996), p. 341.
103 *Livermore Journal*, October 3, 1925, p. 1.
104 *Ibid.*, April 19, 1928, p. 1; May 9, 1929, p. 1; May 30, p. 1.
105 Jensen, John "Jack," recorded interview, Livermore Heritage Guild, May 12,
    1981.

Chapter 7

1 Town Council, minutes, August 5, 1889.
2 *Livermore Echo*, April 2, 1896, p. 2.
3 *Ibid.*, May 14, 1896, p. 3.
4 *Livermore Herald*, May 19, 1900, p. 1.
5 *Ibid.*, May 16, 1930, p. 1.
6 *Ibid.*, May 23, 1930, p. 1.
7 *Ibid.*, June 13, 1930, p. 1.
8 *Ibid.*, editorial, January 2, 1932, p. 2.
9 *Ibid.*, April 1, 1932, p. 8.
10 *Ibid.*, October 11, 1929, p. 1.; *Livermore Journal*, November 22, 1928, p. 6.
11 *Livermore Herald*, February 5, 1932, p. 1.
12 Hagemann, Herbert, oral history transcript, Livermore Heritage Guild (1985), p. 17.
13 *Ibid.*, p. 9.
14 *Livermore Journal*, September 21, 1928, p. 1.
15 Hagemann, Herbert, oral history transcript, Livermore Heritage Guild (1985), p. 14.
16 Homan, *Historic Livermore, California, Illustrated, A–Z* (2007), p. 424.
17 *Livermore Herald*, June 22, 1912, p. 2.
18 Hagemann, Herbert, oral history transcript, Livermore Heritage Guild (1985), p. 12.
19 *Ibid.*, p. 4.
20 *Ibid.*, p. 16.
21 *Ibid.*, p. 8.
22 *Livermore Herald*, January 15, 1910, p. 3.
23 *Ibid.*, December 9, 1916, p. 3.
24 *Ibid.*, December 9, 1916, p. 3.
25 *Ibid.*, October 3, 1925, p. 3.
26 *Ibid.*, April 27, 1918, p. 4.
27 *Ibid.*, July 5, 1919, p. 1.
28 *Ibid.*, May 29, 1925, p. 2.
29 *Ibid.*, May 2, 1924, p. 1.
30 *Ibid.*, March 7, 1930, p. 1.
31 *Ibid.*, March 14, 1930, p. 1.
32 Hagemann, Herbert, oral history transcript, Livermore Heritage Guild (1985), pp. 14-17.
33 Siig, Anna, personal communication with author, 2023.
34 Concannon, James, personal communication with author, 2023.
35 Nebo, William, personal communication with author, 2024.
36 *Livermore Herald*, January 4, 1913, p. 4.
37 *Ibid.*, February 15, 1919, p. 1.
38 Moir, Ralph, personal communication with author, 2024.
39 *Livermore Herald*, April 21, 1933, p. 4.
40 *Ibid.*, June 12, 1936, p. 1.
41 *Ibid.*, July 31, 1931, p. 1.
42 Santucci, Francis May Baer, recorded interview, Livermore Heritage Guild (1982).
43 *Livermore Herald*, June 9, 1933, p. 5.
44 *Ibid.*, January 7, 1944, p. 2.

45 *Ibid.*, April 19, 1935, p. 4.
46 *Ibid.*, September 30, 1938, p. 8.; October 21, 1938, p. 3.
47 *Ibid.*, November 25, 1938, p. 1.
48 *Ibid.*, July 8, 1927, p. 6.
49 *Ibid.*, March 6, 1931, p. 1.
50 *Ibid.*, March 27, 1931, p. 1.
51 *Ibid.*, April 29, 1938, p. 1.
52 *Ibid.*, October 18, 1940, p. 1.
53 *Ibid.*, September 26, 1940, p. 8.; October 3, 1940, p. 1.
54 *Ibid.*, February 24, 1933, p. 1.; March 3, 1933, p. 8.
55 *Ibid.*, July 28, 1939, p. 5.
56 *Ibid.*, December 15, 1931, p. 1.; January 12, 1940, p. 1.
57 *Ibid.*, November 15, 1940, p. 1.
58 *Ibid.*, January 24, 1941, p. 1.
59 *Ibid.*, January 23, 1943, p. 6.
60 *Ibid.*, April 10, 1942, p. 1.
61 *Ibid.*, July 25, 1944, p. 1.

Chapter 8

1 Klein, *Union Pacific, Vol. 2* (2006), pp. 258-278.
2 Dunscomb and Stindt, *Western Pacific Steam Locomotives, Passenger Trains, and Cars* (1980), pp. 12-13.
3 *Livermore Herald*, February 21, 1930, p. 1.
4 DeNevi, *The Western Pacific* (1978), p. 80.
5 *Livermore Herald*, January 8, 1943, p. 2.
6 *Ibid.*, January 22, 1943, p. 1.
7 *Ibid.*, November 24, 1944, p. 6.
8 *Ibid.*, November 30, 1956, p. 14.
9 Dunscomb and Stindt, *op. cit.*, pp. 306-307; Diebert and Strapac, *Southern Pacific Steam Locomotive Compendium* (1987), pp. 24-25.
10 *Livermore Herald*, February 17, 1961, p. 1.
11 Saunders, *Merging Lines* (2001), pp. 213-216.
12 Frank, *Parallel Paths* (2022), pp. 113-114.
13 *Livermore Herald*, May 11,1923, p. 1; August 3 and 10, 1923, p. 1; November 9, 1923, p. 1; December 28, 1923, p. 1.
14 Hayes, *Western Pacific Depots and Stations* (2007), pp. 122-123.
15 *Livermore Herald*, September 23, 1968, p. 1.
16 Shirley, *I Remember: Stories of a Small Town Politician in Livermore, CA During the 1950s and 1960s* (2019).
17 *Livermore News*, November 28, 1961, p.1; December 12, 1961, p.1.
18 Livermore City Council, minutes, May 26, 1966.
19 *Livermore Herald*, January 2, 1962.
20 *Ibid.*, October 6, 1961, p. 21.
21 *Ibid.*, October 13, 1967, p. 1; December 20, 1967, p. 2.
22 *New York Times*, April 9, 1979, Section D, p. 1.
23 Bender, *Southern Pacific Lines Standard-Design Depots* (2013), p. 125.
24 City of Livermore California, Resolution of the City Council (1970), pp. 44-70.
25 Livermore City Council, minutes, August 21, 1972, p. 25 and 373-376; continued August 28, 1972, p. 25 and 380-385.

26 *Tri-Valley Herald*, August 11, 1972, p. 1.

27 *Livermore Herald and News*, September 24, 1972, p. 1.

28 *New York Times*, March 4, 1970, p. 1.

29 Salsbury, *No Way To Run A Railroad* (1982), p. 187; and Saunders, *Merging Lines: American Railroads, 1900–1970* (2016), pp. 379-414.

30 Rail Passenger Service Act, 49 U.S.C. 1 P.L. § 91-518 (1970).

31 Thomas, *Reprieve for the Iron Horse: Amtrak* (1973), pp. 38-42.

32 Railroad Revitalization and Regulatory Reform Act, 45 U.S.C 801 § 94-210 and § 96-448 (1976).

33 *Livermore Herald and News*, July 3, 1973, p. 1.

34 *Ibid.*, August 14, 1973, p. 1.

35 *Ibid.*, February 24, 1973, p.1.

36 City Council, minutes, February 26, 1973, CM 26-199.

37 *Ibid.*, March 26, 1973, CM 26-256.

38 *Livermore Herald and News*, April 10, 1973, p. 1.

39 Letter from Southern Pacific Transportation to Mrs. Ralph (Janet) Newton, May 16, 1973.

40 *Livermore Independent*, June 29, 1973, p. 1.

41 Name withheld to protect source, personal discussion with author, 2022.

42 City Council, minutes, June 25, 1973.

43 *Livermore Herald and News*, June 28, 1973, p. 1.

44 Schrader, telephone and email communication with author, May 10, 2016; meeting, June 22, 2016.

45 Letters between Southern Pacific Development Corporation and city manager, July 17, 1973 and August 19, 1973.

46 Frank, *Depot* (2019), pp. 56, 58-59.

Chapter 9

1 Hiltzik, *Big Science* (1915), p. 353.

2 *Livermore Herald*, June 6, 1947, p. 1.

3 Homan, *Historic Livermore, California, Illustrated, A–Z* (2007), p. 474.

4 *Livermore Herald*, December 14, 1987, p. 1.

5 *Valley Times*, August 30, 1988, p. 1.

6 *Livermore Herald*, May 16, 1952, p. 7.

7 *Ibid.*, September 13, 1919, p. 1.

8 Homan, *op. cit.*, pp. 360-363.

9 *Livermore Independent*, June 20, 2014.

10 *Livermore Herald*, October 8, 1948, p. 1.

11 *Ibid.*, November 5, 1948, p. 4.

12 *Livermore News*, April 16, 1957, p. 5.

13 *Livermore Herald*, May 1, 1953, p. 1.

14 *Livermore News*, November 14, 1955, p.2.

15 *Livermore Herald News*, July 19, 1963, p. 3.

16 Homan, *op. cit.*, p. 481.

17 *Livermore Herald*, February 27, 1942, p. 1.

18 *Livermore Herald*, October 21, 1938, p. 1.

19 Homan, *op. cit.*, pp. 410-412.

20 *Livermore Independent*, May 6, 1973, p. 1.

21 *Livermore News*, October 6, 1959, p. 3.

22 *Livermore Herald*, August 4, 1961, p. 5.

23 *Livermore Herald and News*, February 27, 1963, p. 1.

24 *Livermore News*, September 2, 1954, p. 4.

25 Homan, *op. cit.*, p. 410.

26 *Livermore Independent*, June 20, 2014. p. 4.

27 Gandolfo, Anita, video interview, Livermore Heritage Guild (2023).

28 *Livermore News*, January 17, 1961, p. 1.

29 *Ibid.*, May 10, 1961, p. 1.

30 Homan, *op. cit.*, pp. 482-483.

31 *Ibid.*, p. 108-110.

32 *Livermore Herald*, January 10, 1958, p. 11.

33 Siig, Anna, personal conversation with author (2023).

34 Nebo, William, personal conversation with author (2024).

35 *Livermore Herald*, October 14, 1958, p. 1.

36 *Ibid.*, September 28, 1945, p. 1.

37 *Ibid.*, May 3 1957, p. 1.

38 *Livermore News*, January 17, 1961, p. 1.

39 *Ibid.*, May 10, 1961, p.1.

40 Livermore City Council, minutes, April 20, 1953.

41 *Ibid.*, March 14, 1955.

42 *Ibid.*, August 19, 1956.

43 *Ibid.*, August 6, 1957.

44 *Livermore Herald*, March 28, 1958, p.1.

45 Livermore City Council, minutes, September 2, 1958.

46 *Ibid.*, March 16, 1959.

47 *Livermore News*, September 19, 1961, p. 2.

48 *Valley Times*, July 5, 1990, p. 3.

49 *Ibid.*, *Valley Times*, July 11, 1990, p. 1.

50 *Ibid.*, *Valley Times*, March 15, 1991, p. 1.

51 United States Federal Rule 84-627 (1956).

52 Livermore City Council, minutes, September 16, 1968.

53 *Ibid.*, September 30, 1968.

54 *Ibid.*, November 12, 1968.

55 *Ibid.*, November 10, 1969.

56 *Livermore Herald*, March 29, 1946, p. 4.

57 *Livermore News*, May 5, 1959, p. 2.

58 *Ibid.*, January 6, 1959, p. 4.

59 Bronzen, personal conversation with author, February 12, 2024.

60 *Livermore Herald and News*, February 24, 1964, p. 1.

61 *Ibid.*, August 5, 1964, p. 1.

62 *Ibid.*, March 29, 1975, p. 1.

63 Livermore City Council, minutes, July 23, 1973.

64 *Tri-Valley Herald*, April 21, 1974, p. 1.

65 County of Alameda, Grant Deed, 1974-091689 (1974).

66 Frank, *Depot* (2019), pp. 5-6, 58-59.

67 Alameda County, Assignment of Lease from Southern Pacific Development Corporation to Liaho West, Inc., May 15, 1974 to Great American Restaurants, Inc., 1976-212605, November 24, 1976.

68 *Tri-Valley Herald*, August 19, 1979, p. 2.

69 Alameda County, Amendment to Memorandum of Lease and Consent of Beneficiary, 1979-200458, *Valley Times*, June 22, 1980, p. 19.

70 Pann, *The Life and Times of a Southern Pacific Train Depot in the City of Livermore*, Livermore Heritage Guild (1987).

71 Alameda County, Assignment and Assumption of Ground Lease, 2007-235166.

72 Alameda County, Grant Deed, SPD to Bley, December 30, 1983-247009.

73 *New York Times*, December 24, 1983, p. 29.

74 Alameda County, Grant Deed, 1983-247013; 247014.

75 Alameda County, Grant Deed, 1989-177344.

Chapter 10

1 Nebo, William, personal communications with author (2024).

2 Brown, personal communications with author (2024).

3 Altamont Corridor Express (ACE), *Sacramento Extension Environmental Report, Vol. 2*, September 2020.

4 Valley Link, *Environmental Impact Report, California State Clearinghouse No. 2018092027*, April 2021.

5 Livermore Town Halls, Chapters of Livermore, Livermore Heritage Guild.

6 Jensen, John "Jack," recorded interview, Livermore Heritage Guild, May 12, 1981.

7 Roberts, personal communications with author (2024).

8 Marchand, personal communications with author (2024).

9 *New York Times*, December 24, 1983, p. 29.

10 Alameda County, Grant Deed, 2005-203324 (2005).

11 Livermore City Council, minutes, October 30, 2006.

12 City of Livermore, Resolution 2007-096 (2007), and City of Livermore Redevelopment Agency, Resolution RA-2007-2 (2007).

13 Alameda County, Grant Deeds, 2008-180843, 2008-327044 (2008).

14 Alameda County, Assignment and Assumption of Ground Lease, 2007-235166 (2007).

15 Owens, *Surburbia* (1973).

16 National Public Radio, "Century Light Bulb," June 10, 2001.

17 Hausberg, personal communication with author (2024).

18 *Livermore Independent*, November 7, 2013.

19 *Ibid.*, March 20, 2014.

20 *Ibid.*, June 12, 2024.

21 Brown, personal communication with author (2024).

22 Murray and Raney, *Livermore, The Film*, available at Livermore Heritage Guild and on YouTube.

23 *Livermore Independent*, April 8, 2010.

24 *Ibid.*, April 8, 2010.

25 BBC News, "Crash of the *Nine O Nine*," October 2, 2019.

26 Foster, comments as Rotary speaker, April 3, 2024.

BIBLIOGRAPHY

Ambrose, S., *Nothing Like It in the World* (New York: Simon & Schuster, 2000)

Bancroft, H. H., *The Native Races* (A. L. Bancroft & Company, San Francisco, 1883, Available online)

Bain, D. H., *Empire Express* (New York: Viking Penguin, 1999)

Bender, H. E. Jr., *Southern Pacific Lines Standard Design Depots* (Wilton, California Signature Press, 2013)

Bolton, H. E., *Fray Juan Crespi, Missionary Explorer on the Pacific Coast, 1769–1774, Vol. 2* (Berkeley, University of California Press, 1927)

Brewer, W. H., *Up and Down California in 1860–1864* (University Oxford University Press, London, 1993)

Bronzan, R. A., *A Historical Study of the Livermore Valley Joint Unified School District* (California State University, master's thesis, 1973)

Bryant, E., *What I saw in California* (D. Appleton & Co., 1848, New York Public Library)

Burnham, A., *History & Geology of Livermore Oil* (Livermore Heritage Guild, 2018)

California State Gazetteer and Business Directory (R. L Polk, San Francisco, 1888)

Chiu P., *Chinese Labor in California, 1850–1880: An Economic Study* (University of Wisconsin, Madison, 1963)

Cook, S. F., *The Aboriginal Population of Alameda & Contra Costa Counties, California* (Writat LLC, Casper, 2022)

County of Alameda, California, Official Public Records Portal, Clerk-Recorder's Office, Oakland, Calif., www.ac.gov

City of Livermore, Approved Minutes of the City Council (Livermore Web Public Records Online)

Cottrell, S., *It took 92 years for California to ratify the 15th Amendment* (Grass Valley *Union*, 2020 and 2023)

Deverell, W., *Railroad Crossing* (University of California Press,1994)

Diebert, T. S. and Strapac, J. A., *Southern Pacific, Steam Locomotive Compendium* (Shade Tree Books, 1987)

Dotson, I., *San Ramon Branch Line of the Southern Pacific* (Museum of the San Ramon Valley, 1991)

Drummond, G. B., *William M. Mendenhall, The Story of the Founder of the town of Livermore, California* (Livermore Heritage Guild, 1996)

Dunscomb, G. and Sindt, F., *Western Pacific Steam Locomotives, Passenger Trains and Cars* (self-published, 1980)

Engelhardt, Z., *The Missions and Missionaries of California* (University of Texas, 1915)

Evans, C. W., *Collis Potter Huntington* (The Mariners' Museum, 1954)

Fickewirth, A., *California Railroads* (Golden West Books, 1992)

Frank, Alan M., *Depot* (2019; Parallel Paths, 2022, available from LHG)

Gifford, E. W., Miwok Cults (University of California, 1926, available online)

Gould, L. L., *The Presidency of Theodore Roosevelt* (Oxford University Press, 2012)

Guild, L. H., *Early Livermore* (Arcadia Publishing, 2006)

Halley, Wm., *Centennial Yearbook of Alameda County, Oakland* (1876)

Hayes, S. M., *Western Pacific Depots and Stations* (Hayes Publishing, 2007)

Hiltzik, M., *Iron Empires, Robber Barons, Railroads and the Making of Modern America* (Houghton Mifflin Harcourt, New York 2020)

Hiltzik, M., *Big Science* (Simon & Schuster, New York, 2015)

Hittell, T. H., *The Adventures of James Capen Adams, Mountaineer and Grizzly Bear Hunter of California* (C. Scribner & Sons, New York, 1911); *Hutchings Magazine* (1859)

Homan, A. M., *Historic Livermore, California, A–Z* (Hardscratch Press, 2007, available from LHG)

Johnston-Dodds, K., *Early California Laws and Policies Related to California Indians* (California State Library, 2002)

Judah, T. D., *A Practical Plan for Building the Pacific Railroad* (1857); reprinted as *Judah the Dreamer* (Western National Parks Association, 2001)

Klein, M., *The Life & Legend of Jay Gould* (Johns Hopkins University Press, 1985)

Klein, M., *Union Pacific* (University of Minnesota Press, 2006)

Kleineke, J. A., and Drummond, G. B., 125 Years, *A History of the First Presbyterian Church* (Camino Press, 1955)

Lavender, D., *The Great Persuader* (Doubleday, New York, 1970)

LeConte, J., *A Journal of Ramblings* (Sierra Club, 1960)

Low, F. F. and Becker, R. H., *Some Reflections of an Early California Governor, From an Interview Between Governor Low & Hubert Howe Bancroft in 1883* (Grabhorn Press, 1959)

Margolin, M., *The Ohlone Way* (Heyday Books, 1978; reprinted 2014)

McCullough, D., *The Path Between the Seas* (Simon & Schuster, New York, 1977)

Middleton, W. D., *When the Steam Railroads Electrified* (Indiana University Press, 2001)

Morgenthau, H., *All in a Lifetime* (Doubleday, New York, 1922)

Mosier, D., and Williams, E., *History of Tesla, Second Edition* (Mines Road Books, 2002, available from LHG)

Myrick, D., Western Pacific, *The Last Transcontinental Railroad, Colorado Rail Annual No. 27* (Colorado Railroad Museum, 2006)

National Archive, College Park MD, Original Bond Maps of WP signed by Federal *Inspector* (Record Group 49, Stack Area 331, Tube 67, 1869)

Newton, J., *Las Positas* (self-published, 1969, available at LHG)

Norris, F., *The Octopus* (New York: Doubleday, 1901)

Oliver, D. J., *Hill: Transforming the American Northwest* (Foundation for American Education, 2001)

Orsi, R., *Sunset Limited* (University of California Press, 2005)

Owens, B., *Surburbia* (Straight Arrow Press, 1973)

Ping Chiu, "Chinese Labor in California, 1850–1880: An Economic Study," State Historical Society of Wisconsin for the Dept. of History, University of Wisconsin, Madison, WI, 1963

Rayner, R., *The Associates* (Norton, New York, 2008)

Robertson, D. B., *Encyclopedia of Western Railroad History, Vol. 5, California* (Caxton Printers, 1998)

Salsbury, S., *No Way to Run A Railroad* (McGraw-Hill, New York, 1982)

Saunders, R. A., *Merging Lines* (Northern Illinois University Press, 2001)

Schrader, B., *Will the Last Person Leaving Livermore Please Unscrew the Bulb In Fire Station One* (Livermore Grape Press, 1990)

Shirley, J., *I remember: Stories of a small-town politician in Livermore CA during the 1950s and 1960s* (Camino Press, 2019)

Signor, J., *Southern Pacific's Western Division* (Signature Press, 2003)

Snell, J. B., *Early Railways* (Octopus Books Limited, London, 1972)

Stiles, T. J., *The First Tycoon: The Epic Life of Cornelius Vanderbilt* (Alfred A. Knopf, New York, 2010)

Stover, J. F., *Historical Atlas of the American Railroads* (Routledge, New York, 1999)

Thomas, W. E., *Reprieve for the Iron Horse* (Clator's Publishing, 1973)

Thompson and West, *Official and Historical Atlas of Alameda County, Oakland, CA* (1878)

Tutorow, N. E., *The Governor: The Life & Legacy of Leland Stanford* (Arthur H. Clark Co., 2004)

United States War Department, Reports of explorations and surveys, to ascertain the most practicable and economical route for a railroad from the Mississippi River to the Pacific Ocean. Vol. 5, Part 1 (Washington, D.C., 1855)

Valley Link, Environmental Impact Report (California State Clearinghouse No. 2018092027, 2021)

White, R., *Railroaded* (Norton, New York, 2011)

Withers, B., *The President Travels by Train* (Walsworth Publishing, 1996)

Wood, M. W., *History of Alameda County* (self-published, 1883)

Historic Livermore newspapers indexed by the late Barbara Bunshah. Microfilm copy of papers at Livermore Heritage Guild and Livermore Public Library:

The Livermore Echo
Livermore Enterprise
Livermore Independent, online newspaper references
Livermore News
Livermore Herald, later *Herald and News*, *Tri-Valley Herald*
Valley Times

Other newspapers referenced from University of California collection (cdnc.ucr.edu/>):

Daily Alta California (San Francisco)
Daily Evening Herald (Stockton)
Sacramento Daily Union
San Jose Mercury-News
San Francisco Chronicle
Stockton Daily
Stockton Independent
New York Times

ABOUT THE AUTHOR

Alan Frank is the City of Livermore's historian and a member of the Livermore Heritage Guild. He has been making presentations on the railroad history of the Livermore area to both the city and local Rotary clubs. He was the historic consultant to the City of Livermore for the rescue and refurbishment of the 1892 Central Pacific Railroad Depot. He retired as historian and curator of the Niles Canyon Railway, where he was responsible for placing that segment of the original Transcontinental Railroad on the National Register of Historic Places. Alan retired as a physicist from Lawrence Livermore National Laboratory and was awarded the MIT Edgerton Prize for high-speed photography. He served as a musician with and president of the Livermore-Amador Symphony and is a long-time member of the Rotary Club of Livermore. He is married and has a married daughter with two grandchildren living in Scotland.